DANIEL PLOOF

DISTANT
FROM GOD

Why The
STRUGGLE
To
PRAY
Is Real

Psalm 51
PUBLISHING
GALLATIN, TENNESSEE

Psalm51
PUBLISHING

Library of Congress Control Number: 2025915588

ISBN: 978-1-966758-00-6 (print)
ISBN: 978-1-966758-01-3 (e-book)
ISBN: 978-1-966758-02-0 (audio)

Scripture quotations are from the ESV® Bible (The Holy
Bible, English Standard Version®), © 2001 by Crossway, a
publishing ministry of Good News Publishers. Used by
permission. All rights reserved.

Cover Design: German Creative
Cover Image: Malte Schmidt
Book Editor: Jada Ploof

To Amber, my loving bride.

Thank you for never giving up on me
when I struggled to lead our family in prayer.

You inspire me to be a more godly man.

CONTENTS

Foreword   7

Preface   11

Introduction   13

Day 1   Excuse: DOUBT   17

Day 2   Remedy: FAITH   21

Day 3   Excuse: BUSYNESS   25

Day 4   Remedy: PERSPECTIVE   29

Day 5   Excuse: ARROGANCE   33

Day 6   Remedy: SURRENDER   37

Day 7   Excuse: CONFUSION   41

Day 8   Remedy: INTERCESSION   45

Day 9   Excuse: EXHAUSTION   49

Day 10   Remedy: REST   53

Day 11   Excuse: FORGETFULNESS   57

Day 12   Remedy: PRIORITY   61

Day 13   Excuse: INSECURITY   65

Day 14   Remedy: AFFIRMATION   69

Day 15   Excuse: DISTRACTIONS   73

Day 16   Remedy: INTENTIONALITY   77

Day 17   Excuse: PROCRASTINATION   81

Day 18   Remedy: DISCIPLINE   85

Day 19   Excuse: SHAMEFULNESS   89

Day 20   Remedy: REVERENCE   93

Day 21	Excuse: CYNICISM	97
Day 22	Remedy: PATIENCE	101
Day 23	Excuse: HOPELESSNESS	105
Day 24	Remedy: COMFORT	109
Day 25	Excuse: DISTANCE	113
Day 26	Remedy: INTIMACY	117
Day 27	Excuse: REPETITION	121
Day 28	Remedy: BALANCE	125
Day 29	Excuse: BOREDOM	129
Day 30	Remedy: REVIVAL	133
Day 31	Excuse: RESTRICTION	137
Day 32	Remedy: VULNERABILITY	141
Day 33	Excuse: WORRY	145
Day 34	Remedy: DISCERNMENT	149
Day 35	Excuse: FRUSTRATION	153
Day 36	Remedy: CONTENTMENT	157
Day 37	Excuse: EMBARRASSMENT	161
Day 38	Remedy: INNOCENCE	165
Day 39	Excuse: BITTERNESS	169
Day 40	Remedy: GOODNESS	173
	Postface	177
	Resources	179
	About the Author	183

FOREWORD

Survivor-Level Soul Talk

As a wilderness survival instructor, I teach people the essential skills they need to survive in wild and unforgiving places. The truth is that the wilderness isn't limited to the woods. Each of us is thrust daily into the wilderness of life. There are seasons of uncertainty, hardship, and challenge. And just like in the backcountry, we need survival skills to make it through.

For the believer, prayer is at the top of that list. Like any skill, it must be practiced, refined, and relied upon, especially when the storms roll in. Not the polished kind of prayer. I'm talking about the real kind. The kind that comes from deep places. The kind you whisper when you're tired, scared, or standing at a crossroads. The kind that isn't scripted, but sacred. It's raw. It's honest. It's survival-level soul talk.

That's why I was honored to write the foreword to this 40-day devotional: **"Distant From God: Why The Struggle To Pray Is Real."** Prayer isn't just a book. It's an invitation into "that" kind of communion. Whether you read this at a kitchen table, in the cab of a truck, or beside a smoky campfire, the truth remains the same. Prayer is the single most powerful survival skill a believer possesses.

For over twenty-five years, I have taught people how to meet their basic needs—shelter, water, fire, and food. But long before I teach anyone how to trap a rabbit or purify creek water, I try to help them understand that survival isn't just about the body. It's about the mind, and it's definitely about the spirit. When you're cold, wet, and alone in the woods, it's not your survival gear that will sustain you. It's your perspective. And for the follower of Jesus Christ, that perspective is shaped by a life rooted deeply in prayer.

This devotional meets you right where you are. It's not lofty or filled with theological jargon but raw and real. It offers forty simple but profound reflections on prayer with honest examples from Dan's life to help you navigate your wilderness. These reflections guide you on how to approach it, grow in it, and return to it when life gets unpredictably wild. It covers everything from gratitude and trust to confession and waiting. Each day, it gently reminds you that prayer isn't a performance—it's a relationship. A daily, ongoing, open line to the Father who created you, knows you, and loves you.

1 Thessalonians 5:16-18 instructs us: **"Rejoice always, pray continually, give thanks in all circumstances; for this is God's will for you in Christ Jesus."** All of these three disciplines involve a conversation with God. I just wish I had a book like this when I was first learning to walk with Jesus. For years, I thought prayer had to sound a certain way or be reserved for quiet time in the morning. I've since learned that prayer doesn't require a place, it requires a posture—a reverent one.

That posture comes from a surrendered heart. You can pray in a tent, on a mountaintop, in a grocery store, or in a moment of grief. God is always listening. Prayer carried me through the wilderness of a failing marriage. It sustained me through the heartbreaking loss of our precious daughter. It's not just for life's darkest valleys. Prayer also anchors me in the simple, everyday moments. It is the survival skill of life I trust most because God never fails.

As you walk through these 40-days, I encourage you to treat each reading like you would a trail marker. Let it guide you one step closer—not to religion, but relationship. Let it stir something within you that the noise of life may have buried. If you've ever felt like your prayers don't matter, aren't heard, or will never be good enough, this devotional will remind you that God's not grading your words. He's after your heart.

So here's my challenge to you: don't just read this devotional. Practice it. Take the truths off the page and into your real, everyday life. Pray while you drive. Pray while you cook. Pray while you hike. Pray with your kids. Pray even when you don't feel like it. Especially then, because the consistency of small prayers, whispered often, will do more to shape your soul than any spiritual mountaintop moment ever could. Pray without ceasing! Prayer is the ultimate survival guide for the heart, mind, and soul. And in today's world where stress, noise, and chaos surround us, we all need one.

I'm thankful this devotional made its way into your hands. My hope is that it draws you deeper into the wild, unpredictable, and wonderful adventure of walking with Jesus, one honest prayer at a time. Just remember: God is wild!

Creek Stewart
Survival Instructor, Keynote Speaker, Author, TV Host
creekstewart.com | wildgod.org

PREFACE

From Darkness to Light

If you would have asked me which topic I never wanted to write about, prayer would have been at the top of the list. It is not my strength by any stretch of the imagination. I struggle maintaining a discipline of prayer, and my life bears witness to being relationally disconnected from God. The problem is that I have a laundry list of mental hangups which stunt my spiritual growth. Granted, I pray when expected to or called upon, but the desire to seek the Lord on my own or with my family throughout the day is lacking. I have too many questions, not enough answers, and a history of poor spiritual leadership which testifies to why I struggle with prayer.

Why then would God want me to write a devotional such as this? I have wondered that as well. Yet each time I ask, He reminds me that **"Distant From God: Why The Struggle To Pray Is Real"** is where most Christians find themselves, me especially. Personally, prayer intimidates me. I struggle making it consistent, but I know it is critical to deepen my relationship with the Lord. That is why I cannot continue making excuses. Satan has held my mind captive for far too long and I want God to restore the joy of my salvation, just like He did when I first accepted Jesus as Lord and Savior.

Granted, I have taken steps to improve my prayer life, but Satan tends to destroy any progress I make before I become consistent. As such, I must reevaluate my approach to change. For instance, I will never succeed if I simply reprioritize my life but not refill it with healthy, spiritual disciplines. I cannot say God is my top priority and not prove it by my actions. Rather, I must invest my time wisely and avoid making excuses to experience heart revival. **"For where your treasure is, there your heart will be also" (Matthew 6:21).**

I hate to say that my life is an example of weakness in prayer, but it is indeed the truth. I cannot avoid feeling convicted for wasting many years being disinterested, prideful, and rebellious toward God. I could have cared less about prayer. I knew the Bible emphasized its importance, but that did not compel me to change my behavior either. I was too selfish to admit my laziness, so I avoided prayer altogether. As a result, my wife felt isolated because I refused to pray with her, and our children grew up without a godly role model to emulate due to my negative attitude and personal insecurities.

Thankfully, the Lord changed my perspective and exposed my foolishness. Similar to what the prophet Isaiah experienced (Isa. 6), being chosen by God to serve a specific purpose for the kingdom is an honoring yet humbling experience. I have never authored a book on a topic I knew so little about, but God has opened my eyes to the power of prayer in my search for answers and given me a true hunger to make it a priority. Moreover, He has lovingly confronted my excuses and exposed my insecurities so I could finally recognize my foolish pride and reconcile self-doubt.

I have a long way to go, but I am committed to removing the log from my own eye before focusing on the speck I see in others (Matt. 7:3-5). My heart needs Biblical transformation to become a humble, spiritual leader for our family, and prayer must be a hill I am willing to die upon to avoid falling prey to the enemy's schemes. God has been gracious and patient with me for so long, and it is time I take responsibility for my actions, confront my demons, and build a self-discipline of prayer which never ceases. My family needs me to be a selfless, godly leader in our home, and prayer is how I can maintain a close, personal relationship with God till I see Him face-to-face.

INTRODUCTION

Destroying Strongholds

Who does not struggle with prayer to some degree? As a men's discipleship group leader, I can attest that prayer is an issue for most guys I shepherd. I can ask a room of husbands and fathers, "Raise your hand if you feel uncomfortable praying with your wife," and the response is a resounding, "Yes!" Unfortunately, women are not immune to difficulties as well. Far too many Christians do not feel equipped to pray on their own, pray aloud publicly, or even lead their families in prayer at home. Why? What has made us feel so apprehensive toward prayer that we hold firm to excuses rather than remedy the problem?

We know that we should be praying. Prayer is all over the Bible. However, we spend more time justifying why we avoid prayer than taking necessary steps to understand why we make excuses in the first place. We would rather have a trump card in hand, ready to play when our spiritual disciplines are questioned, than lay down our cards and admit we were bluffing the whole time. Truly, we are not nearly as righteous as we claim to be. None of us are worthy to stand before God's throne of grace knowing we have not taken prayer seriously. Therefore, we need the Holy Spirit to convict our hearts so we can overcome the reasons we struggle praying altogether.

God does not want to condemn us for our lack of daily prayer. Instead, He wants us to realize that we are missing out on a prime opportunity to build a personal relationship with Him. We tend to overlook how guilt, shame, and regret are tools Satan uses to enslave us, but God can use them to draw us back to His presence where hope and healing are found. Sometimes, we need a healthy dose of accountability to grab our attention and redirect our hearts toward heaven. The problem is we often feel more condemned by the enemy than convicted by the Spirit, paralyzed by guilt and unable to respond to the Lord's voice.

Condemnation is nothing more than Satan tempting us to give up on prayer. He wants us to acknowledge that we have wasted too much time being lazy and will never change our selfish ways, so why bother? From Satan's perspective, if he can get us to make excuses and justify our rebellion, we will give up fixing our poor behavior. Conversely, conviction is where the Spirit tugs at our hearts and pushes our excuses into the light so we can see the error of our ways. God does not want us to miss out on spiritual revival. Instead, He convicts our behavior to draw us home in repentance.

The Lord wants us to embrace freedom, not slavery, and prayer is the catalyst to revive our hearts and redeem our souls. How then do we overcome our insecurities and reprogram our minds to love prayer? Too many of us are going through the motions and attempting to appease God with minimal effort. We pray when we really need something as opposed to developing a prayer discipline which can sustain us amid the storms of life. As such, we must learn to pray today so we are well-prepared when calamity strikes tomorrow.

Trials are inevitable, yet how we respond is contingent upon training our hearts to lean upon God for wisdom and strength. We could easily default into self-reliance mode and assume we are well-equipped to handle things ourselves, but that is nothing more than pride poisoning our minds. We are only as strong as our relationship with God testifies. Therefore, prayer must be a daily priority. For by no means is learning to pray easy, but it will become less difficult as we yield to the Lord's sovereignty and trust His Spirit.

There are many reasons why we struggle praying, and this devotional addresses twenty of them by providing remedies, inspired by Scripture, to shift our perspective. Sometimes, what we need more than anything is a fresh glimpse into what we have been missing all along. The blessings that await those who prioritize quality time in prayer are immeasurable. To have the Lord's attention when we call upon His name is an honor and privilege, but do we realize it? Even our president would never personally answer the phone if we called the White House, yet the Creator of the universe is readily available whenever we call upon His name. What then stops us from fostering a deeper connection with Him through prayer?

In many ways, our excuses for not praying are nothing more than smokescreens. We would like to believe that prayer is discretionary and disposable, but nothing could be farther from the truth. It is our lifeblood as Christians, providing direct access into the "oval office" of heaven. Think about it! God has no secretary to check His calendar and schedule an appointment for Him to meet with us when it's convenient. Rather, He speaks directly to us when we pray and gives us unlimited time to share our hearts. It is a priceless gift, yet we often fail to appreciate the value of prayer because it is a long-term investment rather than a scratch-off lottery ticket we throw away.

The problem is that if we see no value in prayer, we will not make time for it. Moreover, if we expect God to answer our prayers how and when we prefer, we are not aligning our personal will with His but demanding He grant our wishes. In those moments, we expect Him to sit and wait patiently until we are ready to talk. However, expectations set us up for failure because there is no room left for God's sovereignty when we demand complete control of our lives. True submission is all about willingly relinquishing our rights to the Lord, not assuming we know best at every moment.

If we are sick and tired of being sick and tired with our prayer struggles, what needs to change? In many ways, it begins with an attitude of respectfully bowing before the Lord in reverence. Even when we do not know what to say, the Holy Spirit meets us in our weakness and intercedes on our behalf. Humility demonstrates that we are willing to lay down our pride and deepen our relationship with God. No longer are we held captive by discomfort because He meets us in the valley of despair and lifts our eyes toward heaven in thankfulness for the victory we have in Jesus. In Christ, our insecurities are atoned for and reconciled, enabling us to speak plainly with Him and express all that is on our mind.

The beauty of drawing closer to God is that we are refreshed when we pour out our souls in prayer and receive healing which we desperately crave. God gives us opportunities to purge what is on our minds so we have a blank slate to build a new foundation. Biblical truth is a critical component of prayer because God speaks directly to us in our quiet times. He illuminates our path toward righteousness so we are not tempted to drift off-course. In many ways, prayer is a path towards godliness, paved by the blood of Jesus who died to set us free. What an incredible picture of self-sacrifice which reconciles our hearts to the Father for all eternity!

In turn, let us embrace the path set before us with anticipation for what the Lord has in store to teach us. Prayer may be a glaring weakness in our spiritual disciplines, but God cares deeply about us and wants us to confront our struggles, resist the enemy's stronghold, and journey with Him along the road of redemption. Quality time with the Lord in prayer is truly the missing link to experience revival in our hearts and minds. Thus, we must humble ourselves and allow the Spirit to illuminate our path home to the Father where hope and healing are found.

Day 1 – Doubt

Excuse: I don't see the point of prayer.

"And Peter answered him, 'Lord, if it is you, command me to come to you on the water.' He said, 'Come.' So Peter got out of the boat, walked on the water, and came to Jesus. But when he saw the wind, he was afraid, and beginning to sink he cried out, 'Lord, save me.' Jesus immediately reached out his hand and took hold of him, saying to him, 'O you of little faith, why did you doubt?'"

— Matthew 14:28–31 —

Prayer can be a complicated issue when doubt enters our minds. How should we pray? What difference does it make? Is God really listening? How will He answer? There are many questions we wrestle with concerning prayer, yet we cannot ignore how critical intimacy with the Lord is to our spiritual health. Similar to reading God's Word which cleanses our minds, prayer connects our hearts to the Father. It allows us to express our true thoughts and feelings without fear of judgment. Still, prayer is devoid of value if we believe God is disinterested or indifferent to what we have to say.

Whether or not we care to admit it, the reason many of us struggle with prayer is because of distrust. We doubt God cares or listens to us. We doubt His timing amid our trials. We even doubt He has our best interests in mind when things do not turn out how we think they should. It is difficult confessing how much we question God, but we cannot ignore how much doubt has poisoned our minds to abandon faith in Christ. It can also spread like cancer if we believe God is absent. Therefore, we must pinpoint what triggers our doubt and remedy the problem before we lose further interest in prayer.

My struggle with doubt often hinges upon my misunderstanding of God's sovereignty. For example, I know that God is supremely in control at all times. His wisdom, power, and authority are evident. Come what may, He will accomplish His will and glorify His name regardless of whether I stop and worship Him. As a result, I struggle believing my words have any power to sway His opinion or earn His favor, which may or may not be possible. I often rationalize in my head, "What's the point? His will be done, regardless of whether I pray, so why am I wasting my time (or His) stating the obvious? He already knows what I am thinking and feeling."

The problem is my perspective is short-sided when I doubt the promises of Scripture which remind me how God meets the needs of His children. **"If you then, who are evil, know how to give good gifts to your children, how much more will your Father who is in heaven give good things to those who ask him!" (Matthew 7:11).** Faith is the foundation of my relationship with the Father. I must believe the Gospel wholeheartedly for it to transform my life but also recognize that God is not a genie in a bottle granting wishes instantly. He will not satisfy my sinful desires nor wait at my beckoning call to do exactly as I please. Instead, He guides me along a straight and narrow path because His love for me is everlasting.

Not every prayer request we make is holy. It may not align with the Lord's will for our lives. Sometimes, we cannot see the other side of the horizon nor dangers which lie ahead. Only God has the foresight to know what is best for us, which requires unconditional faith in His sovereignty to guide our path. It also means we must relinquish control and not place expectations upon how, when, and where He should answer our cries for help. Instead, we must trust that no matter the cost, He has our best interest in mind despite the pain and suffering we may experience.

God continually asks me to trust Him. Like a father who assures his son, "Jump! I will catch you," God is pleading with me to step into discomfort and take a giant leap of faith. He knows that I doubt whether prayer truly impacts outcomes, but that is not the point. He wants me to climb out of the boat and fix my eyes on Jesus so I can stop needing to know why I should pray at all. For doubt causes a disconnect between my heart and mind, and it will stunt my spiritual growth if I do not address it immediately.

When Peter climbed out of the boat and began to walk on water, His faith in Christ was so strong that it overpowered fleshly fear. He was aware of the waves tossing about, but that did not matter. Jesus said, "Come!" and Peter followed. Yet when Peter took his eyes off the Lord, doubt took hold and he immediately began to sink. Faith bowed to the idol of skepticism instead of it overpowering fear. As a result, we are wise to step forward in faith without wavering when the Lord tells us to trust Him.

Expectations play a significant role fueling distrust in our minds. For instance, when God does not answer our prayers in the time or manner we expect, Satan provides a stronghold for us to doubt the Lord's goodness. We also forget that terrible things can happen to good people at any time. The challenge is how will we respond when calamity strikes? Is God still good if He does not pull us out of the fire but instead, allows the flames to refine and purify our character?

Doubt has the power to enslave us. It can also be redeemed by God so long as we allow conviction to draw us into His presence through prayer. In the end, God wants us to lay our burdens down at the foot of the cross and take up the yoke of surrender which is easy and light. Jesus is not far away in our hour of need. Rather, He stands beside us in the fire. All He expects in return is for us to talk to Him daily and trust His sovereignty without reservation.

Application

1. What is the purpose of prayer since God already knows what you are thinking and feeling?

2. Who benefits when you pray? Why?

3. Do you doubt the power of prayer? If so, why do you struggle believing? If not, why do you not pray more often?

4. How has doubt complicated or hindered your prayer life?

5. How has the enemy baited you into believing God is absent or disinterested when you cry out to Him in prayer?

6. Give an example of a time when God called you to step out of the boat and trust Him. What happened and what did you learn from the experience?

7. How have expectations fueled doubt in your heart and mind?

Prayer

Lord, I am ashamed to admit it, but I struggle trusting that You always have my best interest in mind. It seems easier to trust my instincts and personal experience than step into the unknown and trust Your Spirit to guide my path. Help me die to assuming I always know better. I know my poor attitude has a direct impact upon my relationship with You. I yield to doubt far more than I ought because I am scared of trusting what I cannot see right in front of me. I no longer wish to do things my way or force You to conform to my personal will. Help me pour out my thoughts to You in prayer and repentance because Your way is always better. I commit to no longer doubt Your sovereignty but embrace it daily. Amen.

Day 2 – Faith

Remedy: If you lack wisdom, ask God.

"If any of you lacks wisdom, let him ask God, who gives
generously to all without reproach, and it will be given him.
But let him ask in faith, with no doubting, for the one who doubts
is like a wave of the sea that is driven and tossed by the wind."

— James 1:5–6 —

Over the years, I have been gripped by the fact that I struggle in my relationship with Christ because I have a faith problem. It seems counterintuitive but doubt often clouds my judgment and tempts me to lose faith more than I care to admit. I know what the Bible says about trusting the Lord's plan and purpose for my life. I am simply too prideful to confess that unbelief fuels my tendency to trust my instincts more than asking God. I am afraid of what He might ask me to do or give up. So, I bypass obedience and lean upon my own understanding because it is familiar and comfortable rather than the wisest choice possible.

The problem is when I think more highly of myself than I ought, I squeeze God out of the equation and trust my instincts instead of the power of His Spirit who lives within me. It is far easier to rest in myself than allow God to illuminate His truth, convict my foolish decisions, and guide my path. I would rather rely upon personal experience because it is easier and more familiar. I do not have to pray and discern the Lord's will for my life if I solely depend on my own knowledge. I can just trust my better judgment because God gave me a conscience to discern right from wrong, which should be enough to help me make good decisions. Right?

Assuming we have no need for wisdom and discernment is very problematic. Without unpacking our thoughts and feelings through prayer, we can rather easily convince ourselves that we know best. Regrettably, emotions can deceive when people tell us what we want to hear instead of what we need to hear. That is why a personal relationship with Christ is so critical to survival. It is our direct line of communication with God when we are locked in a prison cell of self-reliance and need rescue.

Sadly, we do not want to admit that faith is our biggest problem, but our behavior often testifies to blatant unbelief. When we yield to sin despite God providing a way of escape from temptation, we prove that the Bible is nothing more than ink on a page to us. That might sound harsh, but at some point, God's Word must become living and active in our hearts (Heb. 4:12) to avoid making foolish decisions repeatedly. Faith is the key which unlocks the door to wisdom, yet we avoid turning the handle because we fear what is on the other side. Why?

If we are honest, we do not want to hear what the Lord has to say because it will require us to change our train of thought. In our minds, the future is too risky. We would rather cling to dysfunction because it is familiar and comfortable than trust God and take a leap of faith when we cannot see the future. If only we would lay down our pride, trusting Him in seasons of trials would not be so hard. Keep in mind, Jesus never promised a life of luxury to His disciples. Difficulties will surely come! Therefore, faith is the linchpin of our success or failure. For if we do not trust His sovereignty, we will never look to Him for wisdom when we quiet our hearts to pray.

When I look in the mirror, I see a man who wants to maintain control and not yield to the Lord's will. I know my strengths and weaknesses—what I'm knowledgeable about and where I lack good sense. More often than not, I trust my gut, so there is no reason to tell God what I am thinking and feeling because I believe I have things completely under control. I also assume He is okay with the decisions I make because the Spirit lives within me. Surely, He must be on my side, or so I think!

The problem is that my faith is contingent upon God answering me and yielding to my desires. I am unwilling to bend to His will because He must submit to mine! In retrospect, it is convicting to see how desensitized I am to accountability. For example, rather than read my Bible and seek counsel from the Lord, I rely upon intuition and personal experience to guide my steps. Relying on my gut is not wrong, but it does question whether God's Word is my primary source of truth. Sadly, I often trust myself more than Him, and that poor attitude is why I struggle mightily with prayer.

Christians never want to admit they have a faith problem, but do we believe God's Word so fervently that we align our personal doctrine to it? Are we truly confident in its inerrancy to defend what it teaches regarding purity, ethics, and morality? Prayers which hold no Biblical foundation are merely wish lists. They have no surrender, obedience, or submission to Christ in them. A man who does not grasp who he is praying to is simply hoping for the best. He is too afraid to put skin in the game which is evident by his irritable spirit.

Faith is paramount to prayer. It means we fully understand that wisdom is a gift from God because He is the source of all truth. It assures us that His love is everlasting because we understand the Gospel of salvation, the foundational aspect of why we trust Him. If God did not care about us, He would not have sent Jesus to die in our place. Therefore, we have all the proof we need to know He has our best interest in mind. We simply need to trust His sovereign will and never lose faith in Christ no matter the cost.

Application

1. Would you say you have a faith problem? Why or why not?

2. How has self-reliance hindered you from praying to the Lord for wisdom and strength?

3. Do you have a hard time believing God can do something about your problems? Why or why not?

4. Why is faith a pillar of prayer? What does it support?

5. How does your behavior testify that you struggle believing what you read in Scripture?

6. What is the correlation between faith, prayer, and God's Word? Why does it matter?

7. Are your prayers Biblically-grounded or merely wish lists? Why?

8. What more proof do you need to trust God completely? If none, how can you begin to pray without ceasing (1 Thess. 5:17)?

Prayer

Lord, I believe that **"You are the Christ, the Son of the living God" (Matthew 16:16)**. Why then do I doubt that You always have my best interest in mind? You gave Your life as a ransom for me, yet I fail to trust Your promises and pray for wisdom with unwavering confidence. I know that my actions do not always support my faith testimony. For when You call me to trust, I default into self-mode and rely upon my instincts. Please help me trust Your Word and not lean on my own understanding. I have no reason to doubt Your provision. As such, let my faith compel me to pray in full confidence that You always know what is best for me. Amen.

Day 3 – Busyness

Excuse: I have no time available to pray.

"Look carefully then how you walk, not as unwise but as wise, making the best use of the time, because the days are evil. Therefore, do not be foolish but understand what the will of the Lord is."

— *Ephesians 5:15-17* —

How many of us have used the excuse, "I have no time!" and truly meant it? It is a common phrase, applicable in any situation. What it means is that obligations and personal preferences have become higher priorities in our lives. Thus, we are caught in a tricky situation trying to make time for the one thing which needs our attention most. With prayer, time is of the essence. On the one hand, something must give for us to be available for God despite our busy schedules. Conversely, if prayer is not a priority, what does that reveal about the health of our personal relationship with Christ?

Prayer is all about investing quality time. No matter how we slice it, prayer requires that we stop the train and seek counsel from God. In turn, we tune out all distractions which wage war on our psyche because Jesus is our primary focus. Oftentimes, we act as if we can pray and multitask simultaneously. We assume that we are efficient in finding ways to carve out time for God while meeting our desires. However, are we looking for an opening in our schedule to appease Him, or is prayer already locked into our daily routine? Are we filling time slots around God or just trying to make time for a quick chat?

Intentionality is a huge obstacle for many to overcome. I confess that I have not built my daily schedule around quality time with the Lord, and it clearly shows. I expect Him to wait until I am ready to talk and have no issue putting Him on hold indefinitely when my schedule is full. As a result, He often sits in the waiting room of my heart for days or weeks on end. Regrettably, I often leave the Lord sitting idle as I go about my day without the slightest regard for how my disinterest in prayer is shortsighted and disrespectful.

In Ephesians 5:15-17, Paul encourages us to make the best use of our time. God wants us to tithe the first fruits of our schedule to Him because He desires our full and undivided attention. He knows that if we fill our day with an endless checklist of items to complete, we will overwhelm our minds with other things and give Him table scraps in return. Keep in mind, God is not looking to be an appetizer. He is not content with being dessert either. Rather, He demands we make prayer the main course of our daily consumption so that we glean what we need to survive and not die of starvation.

For too long, I viewed prayer as a nice-to-have instead of a need-to-have throughout my life. Somewhere along the way, I lost my appetite for the main course of communion with God, settling for the equivalent of candy and snacks to quench my hunger. I never saw prayer as equally important to feasting upon God's Word. Knowledge did not develop into wisdom because I failed to pray for understanding. I thought I could just read the Bible and get what I needed rather than pray for Him to reveal truth to my heart and mind. **"For the LORD gives wisdom; from his mouth come knowledge and understanding" (Proverbs 2:6).**

Keep in mind, the enemy can take priorities which are important and position them as if they are opposed to prayer. That does not mean our provisional duties are expendable. Rather, we must figure out a time in our daily schedules to devote solely to the Lord. The time of day is insignificant. He simply desires the first fruits of our hearts which requires undivided attention, hunger for wisdom, and a willingness to receive discipline and correction. **"Like newborn infants, long for the pure spiritual milk, that by it you may grow up into salvation—if indeed you have tasted that the Lord is good" (1 Peter 2:2–3).**

It is certainly difficult to hear what the Lord wants to teach us if we are not listening. Distractions surround us daily and can easily monopolize our time if we are not careful. As such, prayer is a spiritual discipline, because we must train our hearts and minds to prioritize God above anyone or anything else. The key is determining when we have the greatest opportunity to focus our attention. Early in the morning when we wake up might be the best solution, whereas waiting till the end of the day when we can decompress may be ideal. Again, the time of day is less critical because success is all about quality.

Personally, I struggle with both. I have not set aside a time slot to pray daily and my consistency is erratic. I typically go straight to my list of requests before taking time to thank and praise the Lord. No wonder I am intimidated by prayer! My priorities are out of sorts because I fail to grasp how critical quality time is to my spiritual health. Nevertheless, that is one reason I endeavored to write this devotional, because time is a struggle I need to fix immediately.

In the end, we cannot justify that time is out of our control. We all have the same 24-hours to spend wisely. The difference between those who possess a healthy prayer life and those who do not comes down to priority. If God is most important, we will make time for Him. It is as simple as that. Our schedules let us know exactly where prayer ranks in our priorities. That does not mean busyness is not a legitimate obstacle, but victory is attainable if we rearrange our daily routine and prioritize the Lord first instead of last.

Application

1. Why are you so busy these days? How important are the people and things which monopolize your time and attention?

2. Do you find yourself searching for an opening in your schedule to prioritize God, or is your daily schedule built around quality time with Him? How so?

3. How often do you leave God sitting in the waiting room of your heart? What impact has that had on your relationship with Him?

4. What changes can you make to tithe the first fruits of your time and energy to the Lord?

5. Make a list of good and bad distractions in your life. What does it reveal about where you invest your time and the opportunities available to prioritize God more?

6. In retrospect, do you truly believe you have little to no time for God? Why or why not?

Prayer

Lord, thank You for the gift of free-will. You do not force me to have a personal relationship with You but give me a choice to make instead. There are so many things I could be doing in a 24-hour span to bring You glory. However, I often yield to worldly pleasures and force You to sit on the sideline of my heart, waiting indefinitely for my time and attention. Please forgive me for being so arrogant to act as if You are an accessory in my life. I would be nothing without You guiding my steps. Help me build my life around quality time in prayer so that You are the central focus of my day. Amen.

Day 4 – Perspective

Remedy: One day is as a thousand years.

*"But do not overlook this one fact, beloved, that with the Lord one
day is as a thousand years, and a thousand years as one day.
The Lord is not slow to fulfill his promise as some count slowness,
but is patient toward you, not wishing that any should perish,
but that all should reach repentance."*

— 2 Peter 3:8–9 —

Quality time with those we love is a precious commodity. Some would consider it priceless. The truth of the matter is we often take the days, weeks, months, and years God provides for granted. We assume time is always on our side, even though tomorrow is not guaranteed. For all we know, our loved ones might not live to see another day. Death often brings that harsh reality into focus because of its unapologetic finality. There are no do-overs when we breathe our last, just as there are no second chances to pray more when the Lord calls us home. In that moment, we have no other recourse but to accept our fate, come what may, in the Lord's sovereign timing.

The challenge is how do we live for today amongst our busyness and not take quality time with the Lord for granted? In many ways, it all comes down to perspective as 2 Peter 3:8 explains. From God's vantage point, one day is like a thousand years, but how does that impact prayer? If we think about it in financial terms, receiving an immediate rate of return of 365,000% is incredible. A return on an investment like that for every $1 spent is unheard of, yet that is the blessing which awaits us when we prioritize quality time with God on a daily basis through prayer.

However, at times, prayer does not feel profitable. For example, when we assume God will answer us in the time we expect and that our will be done according to our selfish desires, we heap bitterness, frustration, and disappointment upon ourselves. Even still, how often have we invested little to nothing in prayer but expected God to bless us a thousand times over? In hindsight, we could have given Him far more, but a penny's worth of time was all we were willing to invest. We considered our offering good enough to appease Him so He might not cut us off from our inheritance.

The sad truth is I have thrown the equivalent of pennies of my time at God, expecting lottery winnings in return. I am ashamed of how pathetic my investment of quality time with Him has been. One would think I knew better considering the trials I have faced throughout my lifetime. I have experienced valleys of despair which brought me to my knees, yet the Lord rescued me from the mouth of the lion on countless occasions. Why then do I yield to laziness, complacency, and disinterest with prayer when He has proven Himself faithful day after day? Am I that naïve to take His abundant blessings for granted without the slightest remorse?

The main problem is my perspective is often short-sighted. I fail to recognize that one day with the Lord is as a thousand years. It is sobering to consider that calculation. 365-days per year multiplied by 1,000 is how Peter describes time from God's holy perspective. 365,000 to 1! Why then do I pass up the chance to receive God's blessings? In many ways, I consider prayer nothing more than a one-to-one exchange at best and a waste of time at worst. How have I lost sight of the treasure which awaits those who build their lives around the discipline of prayer? Does 2 Peter 3:9 not give the reason why God continues to remain patient with me despite my foolish disinterest of what is ultimately at stake?

God does not desire that we perish eternally. Rather, He wants us to avoid the pitfalls of life on this earth. He knows we desperately need Him. The challenge is we fail to remember His faithfulness because we default into self-sufficient mode rather than depend upon Him as our strength. Quality time with God is critical. It is the refueling aspect of our faith whereby we immerse our minds in the absolute truth of Scripture and allow the Spirit to speak to our hearts through divine revelation. As a result, we pray to receive wisdom, counsel, and discernment for the trials which await us because God hears our cries for help and will meet our needs.

As I have endeavored to compose this book, I am humbled by how the Spirit has illuminated conviction and shown me the error of my ways. While 2 Peter 3:8-9 pertains to the second coming of Christ, it also teaches me that God's math is different from my own. The Lord continually encourages me to remain patient when my flesh demands immediate answers—to trust His sovereignty and not impose my will upon His with non-negotiable demands. How then can I preach the Gospel to my heart on a daily basis and filter out worldly expectations if I am not spending quality time in Bible study and prayer?

Busyness will always be an obstacle to the discipline of prayer in our lives. The enemy knows how susceptible we are to drift from the Lord's safety and security. In turn, Satan strategically isolates our minds and baits us into assuming prayer is a nice-to-have, not a need-to-have. Yet, when we consider that one day with the Lord is as a thousand years (considering the equivalency of that concept from a financial perspective), we understand why prayer is such an intentional focus of the enemy. Satan knows that the more time we spend with God in prayer, the more protected we will ultimately be from succumbing to spiritual warfare.

Application

1. What is your overall perspective of prayer? Why does it matter?

2. How does your attitude directly impact your perspective? What power does it have on your prayer life?

3. How would you define the quality of time you spend with God in prayer as opposed to the quantity of time you invest?

4. Do you believe a day with the Lord is as a thousand years? Why or why not?

5. How can you begin to view quality time with the Lord from the perspective of 2 Peter 3:8-9?

6. Why is prayer an incredible investment of time and energy?

7. Do you consider quality time with the Lord as a sacrifice or an investment? What difference does it make?

8. How is spiritual warfare impacted by the quantity and quality of time spent with God in prayer?

Prayer

Lord, what a difference a day makes! I have read in Your Word that a day with You is as a thousand years, but I never took time to understand what it meant and how it can change my prayer life. My perspective has been so naïve and short-sided. Please forgive me for not recognizing the true value of my time with You. I commit to make You my #1 priority rather than just another item to check off my list of things to do. You deserve far better. Thank You for being patient despite my failures and providing countless opportunities for me to change my foolish ways. Amen.

Day 5 – Arrogance

Excuse: I'm good. I don't need to pray.

*"For by the grace given to me I say to everyone among you
not to think of himself more highly than he ought to think,
but to think with sober judgment, each according to
the measure of faith that God has assigned."*

— *Romans 12:3* —

It is one thing to struggle with why we should pray. It is a whole different issue to determine prayer is somehow beneath us or that we have no need for it altogether. Very few of us believe prayer is a complete waste of time. We are far too sophisticated to declare, "God, I don't need you!" Our rebellion is more discreet than that. However, we let our arrogance speak for itself when we use every excuse in the book to sidestep the fact that pride is ultimately fueling our decisions. In essence, we assume that because everything seems to be going well, prayer is unnecessary or irrelevant. Nevertheless, in our arrogance, we prove the exact opposite is true.

If our lives were falling apart, we would quickly cry out to God for help without hesitation. Human nature compels us to escape the trials we face because we do not enjoy pain and hardship. Why then do we hold an arrogant posture and act as if quality time with the Lord is inconsequential? Romans 12:3 is a good indicator that well beneath the surface of our hearts, we think more highly of ourselves than we ought. We rely upon limited knowledge and understanding because waiting on the Lord takes too long. We want a remedy now, so we hedge our bets on what we comprehend rather than wait for Him to act on our behalf.

Waiting on the Lord is difficult despite what Scripture teaches. King David wrote, **"I wait for the LORD, my soul waits, and in his word I hope; my soul waits for the Lord more than watchmen for the morning, more than watchmen for the morning"** **(Psalm 130:5–6)**. No one ever said that patience was easy, though. It is a fruit of the Spirit, which means it is a blessing we receive when we allow God to sanctify us into the image of His Son. Saying we do not need to pray is often a smokescreen for our lack of patience in God's timing. We want instant gratification and waiting on the Lord is too open-ended for us to accept.

Arrogance in prayer reflects shortsightedness because adoration and gratitude are equally important as confession and supplication. We are foolish to believe prayer is nothing more than a wish list to get what we want. The Lord is not a genie in a bottle, for He spoke creation into existence and sent His Son to die on our behalf. Yet, when we lose sight of thankfulness for who God is and what He has done for us, we assume we are masters of our domain and that the work of our brow produces blessing, not Him. Heaven-forbid if we allow such foolishness to take root in our hearts, because lack of perspective is the beginning of arrogance.

I know that I have lost sight of what prayer is all about because I often posture myself above God. I act as if I have the power to change the trajectory of my life, so I move forward, full speed ahead until the wheels fall off, my engine dies, or I eventually run out of gas. At that point, I am more than eager to cry out, "Lord, I need you!" However, up until that point, I am content to lean on my own understanding rather than humble myself, yield control to God, and allow the Spirit to convict my foolish thinking. The truth is I need the Lord more than ever, but arrogance baits me into believing I can survive "just fine" on my own.

It is nonsense to believe we are ever just fine. An attitude like that assumes that life apart from God is satisfying in any way, which is completely false. **"Let us then with confidence draw near to the throne of grace, that we may receive mercy and find grace to help in time of need" (Hebrews 4:16).** Scripture reminds us that Jesus is our true source of comfort, healing, and protection, because we live in a fallen world. All is never good apart from Christ. Thus, we must lay down our pride and relinquish control of our lives to do as He pleases because His blessings are infinite.

Oftentimes, we act as if prayer is a luxury rather than a necessity. We set God to the side as if He were a mutual fund reserved for future benefit, yet the truth is that we need Him every day of our lives, not just in emergency situations. Otherwise, our journey of faith will be stifled and we'll wonder why we feel so tired, alone, and empty. Needing God and crying out to Him in prayer is not a sign of weakness but strength. It signals that we are powerless to do anything in this world apart from His sovereign grace. Our ability to live and breathe is dependent upon Him. Why then do we act as if prayer serves no purpose?

Truly, I need God with every fiber of my being. I need His wisdom to love my wife in an understanding way. I need His strength to provide for my family's needs and shoulder the weight of spiritual leadership in my home. I need His grace and mercy to die to selfish motives so I can serve others like Jesus would. In all things, I need Christ more desperately than ever before because I am nothing without Him. My life has meaning and purpose because of the cross of Calvary. Therefore, I will aim to never forego prayer but lean harder into it. For what I need is surrender, and prayer is my lifeline to Jesus in every way—not because I am worthy, but because He alone is deserving of praise.

Application

1. Do you think more highly of yourself than you ought? How can Romans 12:3 safeguard you from pride and arrogance?

2. What does arrogance look like in your struggles with prayer?

3. How does pride typically manifest itself in your prayer attitude?

4. How have you allowed your mind to justify that you do not need to pray on a daily basis?

5. When someone asks for your prayer requests, do you often act as if you are just fine and remain silent? Why?

6. What are the potential dangers of only praying to God when you are in desperate need?

7. Make a list of reasons why you need God. Considering this list, how can you thank God each day for His sovereign provision?

Prayer

Lord, Your grace is more than enough for me. Thank You for giving me life and showering me with more blessings than I could ever count. I praise You for the gift of Your Word which leads me to righteousness and guards my soul from utter ruin. Help me die to my pursuit of self-sufficiency. I can do nothing apart from Your strength, yet I act as if I can and then reap the consequences of my folly. I do not want to miss even one day of prayer. Therefore, help me build structure and discipline in my life which prioritizes quality time with You above all else. Write Your Word on my heart, Lord, and guard me from assuming I can do anything apart from Your saving grace and mercy. Amen.

Day 6 – Surrender
Remedy: Abide in me, and I in you.

"Abide in me, and I in you. As the branch cannot bear fruit by itself, unless it abides in the vine, neither can you, unless you abide in me. I am the vine; you are the branches. Whoever abides in me and I in him, he it is that bears much fruit, for apart from me you can do nothing."

— *John 15:4–5* —

There comes a point when we all come to the end of our rope. No matter what trials we might face, we all come to the same fork in the road decision of whether to trust God or abandon faith in Christ altogether. The challenge is that a chasm exists between theory and reality. Theory should prove that we will trust Jesus when trials make us feel as if the walls are closing in around us. However, reality tends to prove our theory untrue when life casts us into the lion's den like Daniel or throws us in the fiery furnace like Shadrach, Meshach, and Abednego. How then do we trust the Lord and lean not on our own understanding?

John 15:4-5 provides the antidote for a healthy prayer life. Jesus said, **"Abide in me, and I in you,"** because He knew we were powerless to save ourselves. Keep in mind, we come to Christ for salvation because He is our source of strength. Whatever trials come our way, we remain firm in our faith because eternal rest is found in Him. We overcome self-sufficiency because the power of the cross overshadows fear. For this reason, Jesus taught us to continuously abide in Him, because rest will never come if we break away from His grace and mercy in favor of independence.

What that looks like in prayer is not placing expectations on God when we ask Him to save us from impending trials. It means we surrender to His timing, which is always perfect, and accept that for our ultimate benefit, things may get worse before they get better. That is the hardest aspect of laying down our pride because we want to maintain some semblance of control. We yearn for the ability to determine our own fate and steer our life in a direction we prefer as opposed to what the Lord may have in store for us. The challenge is how should we respond when we pray for one specific outcome but God has something completely different planned?

My wife and I were faced with a similar dilemma early in our marriage. My father-in-law was diagnosed with bladder cancer and we were determined to relocate from where we were living at the time to where he lived 500-miles away. Only a few years prior, I had lost my mother to ovarian cancer, so our minds were focused on moving closer and maximizing quality time with family. To our surprise, there were no viable opportunities to transfer within my company, so I had to look elsewhere for a quick solution. Inevitably, I began searching for outside sales positions and sent my resume to numerous companies.

Unexpectedly, God shut each door as quickly as I could push it open. Nothing came to fruition. The more I searched and applied, the more evident it became that He would not give us the desire of our hearts. The difficult part was that our request was righteous, or so we thought. Granted, we were motivated by a sincere need to care for Amber's father and support her mother, but nothing came to fruition. Frustration began to consume our minds. Why did God not answer our prayers? If physical healing was not in His sovereign plan, why were we prohibited from moving closer so my wife could spend quality time with her father? None of it made sense.

What we learned during our season of trial was that God would not give us the desire of our hearts until we surrendered full control. It had to be on His terms, not ours. We had to trust that if He called us to stay where we were, we would accept our fate and align with His will. At the time, we felt that our prayers were honorable, but God saw hardened hearts and prideful souls who believed we knew better than Him. We had to humble ourselves during that difficult season of life and trust His sovereignty before He would answer our prayers and grant us the solution we needed.

It is never easy giving up control, but we cannot assume that a branch has any chance of survival by itself. A vine provides nutrients which strengthens the branch and allows it to live. From a prayer perspective, it means immersing our minds in the absolute truth of Scripture which teaches us to abide in Christ. God does not give us a checklist of things to do to earn His favor. He simply asks us to trust His unconditional love and hold firm to that decision. **"If you keep my commandments, you will abide in my love, just as I have kept my Father's commandments and abide in his love. These things I have spoken to you, that my joy may be in you, and that your joy may be full" (John 15:10–11).**

No one ever said the Christian journey was easy. Prayer seems like it should be the most natural thing we do on a daily basis. All it entails is having an honest conversation with the Lord. If only it were that easy! Effective prayer requires a posture of surrender to God's sovereignty and a willingness to trust Him when we cannot see the other side of the horizon. The Lord humbles us when we assume that we know best, which means we can choose to abide in Him or go our separate way. The decision is ours, but surrender is always our wisest option if we desire a healthy and abundant prayer life under the protection of God's sovereign will.

Application

1. Why is surrender to God so difficult at times?

2. How do you struggle relinquishing control and trusting God? In what areas are you prone to not let go completely?

3. Give an example when you were cast into the lion's den or fiery furnace. What did God teach you about surrender to His will?

4. How has your prayer life been hindered by a lack of surrender to God's sovereignty?

5. What does it look like to abide in Christ and remain connected with Him to survive spiritual warfare?

6. Do you believe life is meaningless apart from Jesus? Why or why not?

7. How has God denied one of your prayer requests because it was based on what you wanted and not His sovereign will?

Prayer

Lord, surrender is not something that comes easy to me. I like to maintain control over my circumstances because it is comfortable. My issue is that I do not know what to expect when I pray. I know I am supposed to let go of fear and anxiety and trust You, but that feels so open-ended. There are no guarantees with prayer because it is all based on Your sovereignty. Only You know what is best for me, yet I cannot seem to relinquish control and completely abide in the plans You have for my life. Help me cast off doubt and trust that You will never forsake me. I surrender all to You. Please give me strength to abide in Your will all the days of my life. Amen.

Day 7 – Confusion

Excuse: I don't know how to pray.

"Pray then like this: 'Our Father in heaven, hallowed be your name.
Your kingdom come, your will be done, on earth as it is in heaven.
Give us this day our daily bread, and forgive us our debts,
as we also have forgiven our debtors. And lead us not
into temptation but deliver us from evil.'"

— *Matthew 6:9–13* —

The Lord's Prayer is our #1 example of meditation and spiritual reflection in the Bible. It encompasses praise and adoration to the Father and reminds us to surrender our personal will for His omniscient sovereignty. It humbly asks for daily provision to meet our physical needs, mental fortitude, and spiritual nourishment. It also compels us to confess our sins to God while extending grace and mercy to others. Finally, it finishes with a simple request for the Lord to guard us from the evil schemes of the enemy which seek to draw us away from His unending love and protection.

The Lord's Prayer is a great example, but it can become ritualistic if we are not careful. For instance, I grew up Catholic where reciting is commonplace. Where I have struggled is defaulting into recitation mode without reflecting on what I am saying and why I am saying it. Reciting the Lord's Prayer became an easy way to talk to God when I did not know how, but it became the only thing I prayed as well. Rather than praying relationally by inserting my life into the equation, I used the Lord's Prayer to be my "one size fits all" means to an end. Thus, I had to reconcile whether it was a framework for building prayers or merely a recitation exercise to appease God.

One of our greatest excuses for not praying more is a lack of knowledge and understanding of what prayer looks like. We assume that proper structure and expertise are required to earn God's favor and attention. Structure is important to organize our thoughts and focus our attention, but we are not reciting a grocery list of demands to God and nothing else. Prayer should be conversational, which requires that we bring Scripture into the equation so we can hear God's voice more clearly. No relationship can thrive if it is always one-dimensional. Therefore, we must not only talk to God but read His Word to hear Him speaking back to us.

I know that I am easily confused when I fail to bring balance and perspective to my prayer life. If I am running on the fumes of logic and not cleansing my mind with the water of God's Word, I can rationalize anything to be true in my psyche. Satan's ability to confuse me is always dependent upon the quantity and quality of time I spend reading Scripture. If I am meditating on it daily, I am less likely to be led astray by relative truth. However, if the dust on my Bible grows larger with each passing day, the likelihood of me not yielding to temptation diminishes significantly.

For example, a member of my extended family recently attacked my faith because I did not endorse behavior which the Bible clearly condemns as sin. The level of hatred I received took me by surprise. I was not expecting to be persecuted for my faith, but it was also an opportunity to test whether I knew how to pray and hear God's voice speaking in return. In that moment, the Lord gave me wisdom by illuminating my mind with Scripture stored deep within my heart. My flesh wanted nothing more than to retaliate and defend my position, but the Spirit overwhelmed my heart with truth from God's Word and calmed my mind. That enabled me to steady my heart and not sin by reacting in unrighteous anger.

Oftentimes, we believe prayer is all about saying the right thing, which is fine if we have time on our hands to discern what to say. However, calamity usually strikes when we least expect, so we must know how to respond before trials come to not waver in confusion. When life comes crashing down, we learn how prepared we are to handle stress. In those moments, the fire of trials burns away all the impurities of our excuses which forces us to reconcile how ready we are to handle opposition. It is why we need Jesus, because we cannot carry our burdens alone. For He is ready and willing to shoulder the weight for us, but we must relinquish control to Him first.

What the Lord desires is our brutal honesty and true brokenness. **"If we confess our sins, he is faithful and just to forgive us our sins and to cleanse us from all unrighteousness" (1 John 1:9).** Satan would have us believe that our speech must be smooth, our rhetoric polished, and our knowledge of Scripture profound to approach the throne of grace. Yet, nothing could be further from the truth. **"For everyone who exalts himself will be humbled, but the one who humbles himself will be exalted" (Luke 18:14).** As a result, we are without excuse if we act as if we have no idea how to pray when all God desires is a humble heart.

True worship compels us to thank Him for who He is and what He has done for us. As we are overwhelmed by His majesty, we recognize the depravity of our hearts which elicits confession and a plea for Him to protect us from temptation. The Lord's Prayer was never meant to be a cure-all but a blueprint to experience intimacy with our Father in heaven. He wants us to have a personal relationship with Him—bathed in humility, reverence, and brokenness over sin. Therefore, if we lay down our pride we will hear God's voice speaking plainly to our hearts, reminding us not to be led astray by the evil schemes of the enemy but set apart for righteousness' sake.

Application

1. Are you ever confused by how to pray? Why or why not?

2. What are the benefits and detriments (if any) of only reciting the Lord's Prayer when you pray?

3. Are your prayers repetitive in any way? Why or why not?

4. Do you use similar words or phrases when you pray? How so?

5. Do you believe effective prayer should be recited (like the Lord's Prayer) or open-ended? What are the pros and cons of each?

6. What role does Scripture play in your prayer life? What changes do you need to make to wash your mind with the truth of God's Word more often?

7. Why are praise and worship critical to a healthy prayer life?

8. What do you believe God wants you to learn in order to pray more effectively? Why?

Prayer

Lord, I am often perplexed with trials of life. Why am I confused by how to pray as well? Prayer should be effortless, yet I struggle knowing exactly what to say to You. I realize that Satan wants nothing more than to distract my attention and make me believe there is a specific formula I must follow to pray effectively. Yet, what I have learned is that You desire humility and brokenness. Help me to not be intimidated by the eloquence of prayer but rest in the quality time I get to spend with You. Soften my heart to the truth of Your Word so I hear Your voice more clearly. Thank You for being the source of wisdom and discernment in my life, Lord. Amen.

Day 8 – Intercession

Remedy: The Spirit helps us in our weakness.

"Likewise the Spirit helps us in our weakness. For we do not know what to pray for as we ought, but the Spirit himself intercedes for us with groanings too deep for words. And he who searches hearts knows what the mind of the Spirit is, because the Spirit intercedes for the saints according to the will of God."

— Romans 8:26–27 —

How often have we found ourselves in desperate moments of great need, overcome with emotion? There are seasons of life which are so wrought with pain, heartache, triumph, and joy that we cannot find words to express how we feel to God. Those moments are too raw and honest for us to express without weeping. When we open our mouth, nothing comes out, because it is all too real for us to comprehend. How then do we find the right words to pray in times of great sorrow? How can we sing praises to God when tears continue to flow freely? Is there a way to really convey our thoughts and emotions to God when we are physically unable?

Romans 8:26-27 is a wonderful passage of Scripture to encourage our hearts. For in our greatest hour of weakness, when we cannot summon the words to adequately express our thoughts to God, the Spirit intercedes on our behalf. Keep in mind, our Helper (John 14:26) already knows what we are thinking and feeling, so there is no possibility of confusion. We can rest in the blessed assurance that God hears our cries and knows what we need, even before we do. By the power of the Holy Spirit, our Creator searches our hearts and identifies with our struggles which seem too difficult to bear.

What is so powerful about the Spirit's intercession is that we are without excuse before the Lord. No longer are we able to rest on our laurels or justify our lack of spiritual discipline based upon perceived ignorance of not knowing how to pray. In two verses, God destroys our favorite excuse by reminding us that the same Spirit who raised Jesus from the grave lives in us and intercedes for us. What case can we make then to justify our lazy behavior? There is none! God has sovereignly ordained a way for us to communicate with Him even when we do not know how.

Excuses are a dime a dozen. I have used every justification possible to sidestep my responsibility of modeling prayer in my home. At the top of the list is not knowing how to pray. I often point to the fact that my Dad never taught me how. My mother prayed a rosary daily after converting to Catholicism in marriage, yet I never took to praying the way she did. I did not understand the point of recitation. I grew up not knowing there were other ways to pray than reciting "Hail Mary" or "Our Father," but I also never took time to educate myself by reading the Bible either.

Prayer was never relational to me but religious. I was taught to follow a repetitive formula, but I struggled connecting the dots to why I felt so distant from God. For me at least, praying the rosary did not solve my frustration. It only fueled my lack of prayer because I did not understand how it cultivated a personal relationship with God. It was not until I began reading Scripture that I learned how the Spirit intercedes for me despite my ignorance. I no longer had to fear saying the wrong thing. All I needed was to show reverence and respect before the Lord and be honest with Him regarding what I was thinking and feeling.

I will be the first to admit that I am far from being a devout man of prayer. However, the Lord is convicting me that I cannot hold onto the past and use it as a crutch for sidestepping responsibility to pray daily. I do myself no favors banking on the same excuses and expecting my family to somehow benefit from my laziness. God has provided the means necessary for me to conquer my rebellion by giving me an intercessor who speaks on my behalf. What more can I ask for?

That does not mean the Spirit does all the talking when we have no issue speaking to the Father. Romans 8:26-27 encourages us that the Spirit steps into the gap with groanings too deep for words when we are overcome by emotion. There are many occasions when we have experienced the Spirit conveying our thoughts to God in our darkest hours. If we are overcome with depression and unable to control our anxiety, the Spirit intercedes for us. When gratitude for God's blessings compels us to worship Him in reverence, the Spirit also intercedes on our behalf.

The real question is whether we will allow the Spirit to illuminate our minds with the truth of Scripture or quench His voice. Without realizing it, we often expect the Spirit to do everything while we just carve out time in our schedules and do nothing more. No, we must continually discipline ourselves and learn how to pray. We are not alone in our struggle. God is with us wherever we go. He loves us like a Father and intercedes for us in the Spirit realm. How then could we ever doubt His sovereign provision?

He has given us far more than we could ask for or imagine. His love is everlasting and He knows the desires and intentions of our hearts. He knew before creating us that we would struggle talking with Him. As a result, He gave us His Spirit to guide our path so we would know His heart more intimately. God speaks to us through His Word, and by His Spirit, He illuminates truth in our hearts and minds so we can hear His voice more clearly.

Application

1. How is the Holy Spirit's intercession an immeasurable blessing to your faith journey?

2. How has the Spirit interceded for you when you did not know how to pray?

3. If the Spirit's groanings are too deep for words, how are they similar or different from your own?

4. What level of personal accountability does the Holy Spirit bring to your discipline of prayer?

5. Knowing the Spirit intercedes for you, how are you convicted by the effort you typically make to pray?

6. Why is it so easy to fall back on the excuse, "I don't know how to pray," rather than remedy the problem?

7. How does the Spirit illuminate Scripture in your heart and mind so you can hear God's voice more clearly?

Prayer

Lord, You are beyond gracious to me and know what I need long before I do. Before I was created, You knew I would struggle knowing how to pray. You knew I would require help understanding the wisdom of Your Word. Therefore, You sent Your Spirit to sanctify my heart and lead me towards righteousness. Please forgive me for taking Your precious gift for granted. I never realized how glorious it is to have Your Spirit reside in my heart. All I ever need has been graciously provided by Your sovereign hand. Thank You for Your provision, for I am humbled by Your grace. Amen.

Day 9 – Exhaustion

Excuse: I'm too tired to pray.

"Come to me, all who labor and are heavy laden, and I will give you rest. Take my yoke upon you, and learn from me, for I am gentle and lowly in heart, and you will find rest for your souls. For my yoke is easy, and my burden is light."

— *Matthew 11:28–30* —

One of the most honest confessions we could ever make to God is admitting that we are too tired to pray. Exhaustion is a real deterrent to healthy prayer because our focus wavers the more we yield to it. The challenge is that fatigue can be mental, emotional, or spiritual, yet the common enemy we face is the physical tiredness of keeping up with the demands of life. Busyness wages war against the Spirit's conviction to draw us into fellowship with the Lord, but fatigue ensures that even if we do find time to pray, it will be mediocre at best due to sheer exhaustion.

Maintaining focus is one of my biggest prayer struggles. My mind can go from talking to God one minute to thinking about something completely different in an instant. I am easily drawn to tangents and rabbit holes which distract my attention from prayer. The challenge is when I catch myself drifting off and then refocus my attention, I forget what I was originally saying. Guilt and shame also overwhelm my heart because I allow my mind to get off track so easily. In turn, rather than apologize to God for getting distracted, I throw in the towel and give up. In my mind, I rationalize that if I am too tired and cannot focus on talking to the Lord without drifting off on a tangent, what is the point of praying any further?

It is fairly easy to give up on prayer when our bodies need rest and our minds are overwhelmed. We know God deserves the first fruits of our attention. Therefore, if we cannot give Him the quality time He deserves, we are better served catching up with Him later, or so we think. That is the power of spiritual warfare. Satan knows if he can get us distracted and complaining about how tired we feel, we will rationalize why it is better to rest now and pray later. Granted, we may actually need physical rest in extreme instances, but is that truly our norm? Will we get around to praying later or just make another excuse?

The benefit of exhaustion is that it magnifies our need for Jesus and the rest He provides. Matthew 11:28-30 is one of the Bible's greatest passages because it promises eternal rest and relief when we cannot bear the weight of burdens any longer. Jesus understands the responsibilities we shoulder and sympathizes with our weaknesses. He identifies with how we think and feel and beckons us to release our grip on the trials we face. He knows how hard it is to trust that tomorrow will be any different. For He empathizes with our fatigue, which makes it even more amazing that He is willing to trade our yoke of suffering for His which is light and easy.

Desperation is one instance where I have been so crushed by the weight of sin that I had no other choice but to give up control and stop running. The weight of guilt, shame, and regret was too heavy to bear, so I prayed that God would intervene and help me reconcile sins I held onto for so long. For those who have read my 40-day devotional, **"Attributes of a Godly Man,"** I talk extensively about my past struggles with lust and pornography and how my depravity eventually devolved into adultery. In a nutshell, it did not take long for me to recognize my sin, end the affair, and confess my sins to God, but I also ran away and hid from confessing to my wife.

What immediately followed was a long season of dormancy and fear where I went into spiritual hiding. I became emotionally distant and pulled away from the body of Christ because I was too afraid to own my sins and the consequences of my actions. Nevertheless, the Spirit continued to convict my heart because I skipped a key part of the repentance equation. I still needed to reconcile my sins with my wife, Amber. What ensued was an avoidance of conviction. I distanced myself from God for almost two-years until He gave me the opportunity to confess my sins and live in the light of truth.

Eventually, I chose to obey the Spirit. I was completely worn out and exhausted from running away. In His love, God gave me the chance to right the wrongs I committed. It was not easy. I put my wife through pain and anguish as a result of my selfishness, but God met us in that season of desperation. I needed to confess my sins because she deserved to know the truth and ultimately decide whether she still wanted to be married to me. By God's grace, she gave me a second chance because she trusted the Lord, not me. She was mentally, emotionally, and spiritually exhausted, but that only drew her closer to Jesus through prayer, not further away.

Exhaustion comes in many forms and for varying reasons. The question we must reconcile is whether we will continue to run and hide from the Lord or fall down on our knees and worship Him. We all have needs, but the worst thing we can do is bear our yoke all alone rather than accept the priceless offer Jesus makes instead. Our Savior's yoke is easy and light for a reason, and we are foolish to decline His gift when we are so overwhelmed by exhaustion and fatigue that we cannot think straight. Inevitably, the choice is ours. We can continue to do things our own way or surrender our pride at the foot of the cross in humble repentance. One path leads to rest and peace while the other only enslaves us further to self-protection.

Application

1. Why are you so tired these days? What burdens are you bearing that you need to lay at the foot of the cross once and for all?

2. What did Jesus mean when He said, **"My yoke is easy, and my burden is light?"** What difference does it make?

3. How has exhaustion become a bottleneck in your prayer life?

4. Which burdens that you carry daily are self-imposed? How can you learn to relinquish control of them to God?

5. How can exhaustion actually kickstart your prayer life into gear?

6. Why does fatigue magnify your need for God rather than draw you away from His presence?

7. Give an example of how God has ministered to you in a season of exhaustion. What did He teach you through that experience?

8. How do you believe God feels when you admit, "I'm too tired to pray?" How can you guard against using that excuse?

Prayer

Lord, You know how tired I am these days but using fatigue as an excuse is not helping me one bit. The only way I can find rest for my soul is by trusting You and laying my burdens down at the foot of the cross. I cannot seem to avoid shouldering the weight all by myself. I want to believe I am strong enough, but all I prove is how foolish I am to carry an eight-hundred-pound gorilla on my back every day. Break my pride and help me accept the gift of grace You provide in exchange for my exhaustion. I am tired of running from Your Spirit. Help me cling to Your cross of salvation instead. Amen.

Day 10 – Rest

Remedy: In peace, I will lie down and sleep.

"In peace I will both lie down and sleep; for you alone,
O LORD, make me dwell in safety."

— Psalm 4:8 —

How many of us take time to rest? Are we sleeping well and for enough hours to ensure our body functions properly? Do we wake up refreshed or dreading tomorrow because we feel tired and weary? In many ways, our attitude sets the trajectory for how we face demands, navigate trials, and manage expectations. The same goes for our prayer life. How we respond to God through adversity sets the tone for whether we are restless in spirit or eager to learn what the Lord might teach us. The real question is whether we are willing to stop and listen.

There is nothing which tests our patience more than being asked to wait. In our minds, we have things to do, places to go, and people to see. We have no time available to sit for an undisclosed amount of time waiting on God to act. We would rather take matters into our own hands and see what happens. The challenge is we are often consumed by turmoil deep within our souls. Our minds can become so overwhelmed by hypothetical scenarios or what the future might bring that we forgo prayer altogether and hedge our bets on what we think is the best course of action.

Just as David affirms in Psalm 4:8, we must ensure our hearts are resting in a state of peace rather than chaos to hear God's voice speaking. Despite the storms raging in our minds, we must seek shelter in Christ, who encourages us to rest in the eye of the storm.

Logic would tell us to run away if a hurricane were bearing down, yet Jesus assures us there is no more peaceful place to be than in the middle of the chaos, fully dependent upon Him.

In my book, **"Lord, I'm Tired: Gospel Truth for a Restless and Weary Soul,"** I talk about our recent experience in the direct path of an EF2 tornado which significantly damaged our home. The power of a ferocious twister is intense. In a matter of 20-seconds, our roof was torn apart, screen porch destroyed, mailbox uprooted, and windows damaged, among other things. Huddled on the floor of our bedroom closet, there was nothing we could do but pray for the Lord to protect us. We had no way to divert the tornado or steer it away from our home. All we had was the power of prayer.

That is what lying down peacefully in the eye of the storm looks like from a spiritual lens. It conveys that our focus is squarely on Christ and we are oblivious to whatever else is going on around us. Similarly, when Peter jumped out of the boat and began walking on water, his eyes were fixed on Jesus (Matt. 14:22-33). It did not matter that he almost drowned. His ears were not swayed by the sound of thunder rumbling. It was only when he allowed his eyes to veer off course that the enormity of the wind and waves drove him to panic.

It seems illogical to rest peacefully in the arms of Jesus when life feels completely out of control. How can we focus our minds to pray when we are sleep-deprived and burning the candle from both ends? Something has to give! Thankfully, that is when the Spirit reminds us not to run away from our problems but seek the Lord instead. For He knows we are stretched thin and on the verge of a mental breakdown, more so than we care to admit. Therefore, He meets us in our valley of despair. That is also when we discover how trusting God's sovereignty is far easier than attempting to strongarm trials into submission on our own.

There is nothing we can do to avoid trials if the Lord wills that we be tested to sanctify our faith. It does not mean He abandons us in our hour of need. Rather, He sticks closer than a brother, because He knows our dependency will increase if we stop trying to fix our problems and instead, talk with Him in prayer. It is easy to assume trials are meant to isolate us and cause sleep-deprivation, spiritual malnourishment, and dehydration from the living water of God's Word. However, being tested is not intended to reveal our strength and knowledge, but rather to show who God ultimately is to us.

Whether isolated in the wilderness or in the eye of the storm, our dependence on God must exponentially increase if we expect to survive. John the Baptist testified concerning Jesus, **"He must increase, but I must decrease" (John 3:30)**. Thus, the more we lay our burdens down at the foot of the cross, the easier it is to pray. We realize that our strength comes from Him alone which makes prayer more satisfying because we understand that Jesus is all we need. That is the power of dwelling in the shadow of the Most High where we are safe and secure. Depravity is magnified in the valley of despair, but the blood of Jesus is powerful enough to pull us out of darkness and into the light of grace.

It seems easier said than done to simply rest in Jesus. There are no guarantees that if we do, all our problems will magically go away. Nevertheless, spiritual rest is possible when we stop trying to control our circumstances, go to God in prayer, and fully trust in His sovereign will for our lives. That does not mean learning how to rest in Jesus is easy, but it is necessary to experience peace, joy, and contentment on this side of heaven. In the end, we must not worry about the storms of life which continually exhaust us, but rather fix our eyes squarely upon Jesus, the calmer of storms and giver of true rest and contentment.

Application

1. What does it mean to dwell in the safety of the Lord?

2. How long do you typically sleep each night? How has sleep deprivation impacted your ability to pray?

3. What kind of rest do you crave most (physical, mental, emotional, or spiritual)? Why?

4. Which trials draw your attention away from God and consume your mind with fear, doubt, and worry?

5. How can you rest peacefully in the eye of the storm rather than run away from it? Why is it important to your spiritual survival?

6. Knowing that trials are meant to draw you closer to God, how can you consider them with joy rather than sorrow?

7. How can rest revive your prayer life? What changes must you make to experience peace more often?

Prayer

Lord, I praise You for the gift of rest. When I am tired and weary, You fill my cup and give me strength to live another day. What I do with the time You provide is what concerns me most. I do not want to complain about trials I am facing or how they push me to my breaking point. Rather, I want to consider them with complete joy and experience what it feels like to rest in the eye of the storm, fully dependent on You. Help me cast off fear and worrying about what the future entails, and let Your will be done in my life. Apart from You, life is meaningless. Therefore, help me to never forget how desperately I need Your Word every day of my life. Amen.

Day 11 – Forgetfulness

Excuse: I forget to pray daily.

*"If anyone is a hearer of the word and not a doer, he is like a man
who looks intently at his natural face in a mirror. For he looks
at himself and goes away and at once forgets what he was like.
But the one who looks into the perfect law, the law of liberty,
and perseveres, being no hearer who forgets but a doer
who acts, he will be blessed in his doing."*

— James 1:23–25 —

Forgetfulness impacts us all. No matter how old we are, we tend to forget things that are important and remember things which are insignificant. It only gets worse as we age, but are we excused by God when we forget to spend quality time with Him in prayer? Is He satisfied with being deprioritized in our daily schedule? Keep in mind, Scripture clearly states that idolatry is a serious sin to God. **"You shall have no other gods before me" (Exodus 20:3).** The challenge is that what if our intentions are pure, but we simply lose track of time and forget to pray? Is it truly inexcusable for us to not prioritize prayer, even under challenging time constraints?

The difficulty with forgetfulness is that it is easy to rationalize and justify. There may be legitimate reasons why our day took an unexpected turn and monopolized our time and attention, but is that a common occurrence or an exception to the rule? Do we believe any excuse is acceptable to justify forgetfulness, or are we rationalizing our disobedience to avoid admitting that we do not think about God, let alone pray to Him? It is a tough pill to swallow when we admit how selfish we are to prioritize anyone or anything above the

Lord, yet it is necessary to remedy our sinful actions and make positive changes to our spiritual disciplines.

For example, I have a terrible memory. I am the type of person who forgets someone's name two seconds after I meet them. I can also remember key takeaways from a conversation but not specific details. My wife, on the other hand, has the memory of an elephant. She remembers everything! She can have a two-hour conversation with someone and repeat back virtually every detail. She amazes me because I am not wired that way. I wish I could remember entire conversations, but I tend to be a "cliff notes" kind of guy, able to summarize long conversations in just a few sentences.

My biggest problem with forgetting is that I fail to understand the impact it has on others. Needless to say, my poor memory drives Amber crazy. I can see smoke coming out of her ears when I forget what she said a minute prior. It is not a character trait I am proud of, yet it is not something I attempt to fix either. I can only imagine how frustrated God must be when I forget to pray daily. As a parent, it would irritate me if I told my girls to do something and they said, "Okay," but immediately turned and forgot my instructions. I am just thankful the Lord is patient with me despite my bad memory!

The danger of forgetfulness is the lack of concern we convey to God by not remembering Him. How can He be first and foremost in our lives if talking to Him does not cross our minds? We can go days, weeks, or months without praying and not miss a beat, but have we ever put ourselves in the Lord's shoes and considered how selfish we are from His perspective? It should be convicting enough to drop us to our knees and repent of our sins. God gives us free will to pick and choose how we invest our time. The real question is where He ranks in our list of daily priorities.

There is no excuse worthy of condoning selfish behavior. God knows our hearts, so there is no point trying to sidestep accountability to lessen our conviction. When we put God on silent mode, we communicate, "Lord, I don't really need you." That is a harsh reality to own, but there is no justifiable reason to forget talking to Him. Every blessing we receive is sovereignly provided by the work of His hands. How then is He not worthy of endless thanks and praise? **"In his hand is the life of every living thing and the breath of all mankind" (Job 12:10).** What more evidence do we need? He is the supreme giver of life and blessing!

The harsh truth James 1:23-25 conveys is that while we can love and appreciate the Lord, our actions speak louder than our words. We prove where our heart's devotion lies when we pick and choose our daily priorities. Forgetfulness does happen sometimes. That is just a part of living in a fallen world consumed by spiritual warfare and an enemy intent on pulling us away from God. However, more often than not, we forget to pray because we fail to find value in it. Our minds are too focused on instant gratification to see the big picture and long-term effects of prayer and how it guards our hearts and minds from sin and temptation.

I wish I had prioritized prayer long ago because I was once the epitome of hypocrisy. I would look at myself in the mirror, see my sinful depravity, and walk away assuming I was a righteous man. My perspective was actually delusional. I was spiritually blind to my own blindness yet walked around acting as if I could clearly see. I felt as if I did not need to pray, so it became an emergency card in my life. Forgetfulness developed into a habit because I never understood why prayer was essential for survival. Nevertheless, life has taught me lessons the hard way, and I praise God for helping me understand that prayer is the catalyst to lasting peace in my life.

Application

1. Do you believe there is a pressing need to talk to God daily and pray without ceasing? Why or why not?

2. How has remembering to pray daily positively impacted your faith journey?

3. What are some easy ways to avoid forgetting which can impact your spiritual disciplines altogether?

4. What is the overarching impact of forgetting to pray? Why does it matter in the grand scheme of things?

5. When you forget to pray, do you hurt yourself more or God? How so?

6. How have you experienced the harsh reality of James 1:23-25? What have you learned as a result?

7. What regrets do you have about forgetting to pray? Which do you need to confess to experience peace?

Prayer

Lord, intentionality is an issue I struggle with mightily. Forgetting to pray has become a byproduct of disobedience by not making You the central focus of my life. I confess that sometimes I do not want to pray. I am too tired or too busy. What I want to avoid admitting, though, is that I continually forget to make You top priority which is inexcusable. Please forgive my selfishness. Renew a hunger in me to talk with You daily and worship You constantly. You are worthy of praise and I must discipline myself to appreciate Your sovereign provision despite my wandering heart. Amen.

Day 12 – Priority

Remedy: Seek first the kingdom of God.

*"But seek first the kingdom of God and his righteousness,
and all these things will be added to you."*

— *Matthew 6:33* —

Who matters most in our lives? It is a powerful question with enormous ramifications. Certainly, there are people who are important to us, but where does God inevitably fall in our priority ranking? Is He first, last, or somewhere in the middle? The challenge is that actions speak louder than words. We can say God is our top priority, but how we invest our time and energy speaks directly to who or what we treasure most. If God is first and foremost in our lives, we will prioritize prayer and quality time studying Scripture. If anything else takes precedence over this, the Lord will likely take a back seat regardless of whether we intend to put Him there or not.

Matthew 6:33 is a convicting verse. It comes near the end of what Jesus preached in His sermon on the mount regarding anxiety. His remedy to overcome fear, doubt, and worry is contingent upon us seeking the Father first and making Him our sole priority in life. The key to what Jesus taught is that our Creator delights in simplicity. He assures us, "Just trust me. That is all you need to do. Trust me with your life and do not worry about anything else." Nevertheless, we tend to complicate things and then wonder why we feel so dazed and confused.

For example, provision and safety are expectations God places upon us as parents to protect our families. There is certainly nothing wrong with that, but where does our ability to accomplish those tasks come from? Is God not the source? Truly, when we look to ourselves and not the Lord, we assume we can survive without Him. We begin drifting in our faith like a ship lost at sea, not realizing that our decision to move the Lord down our priority list causes far more challenges than we initially thought.

When we lose sight that God alone is our source of strength, we deprioritize prayer because we see no value in it. Thus, it is imperative we seek God's kingdom and avoid pushing prayer down our priority list. There is nothing we do which communicates spiritual arrogance more than acting as if we do not need the Lord unless it is an emergency. His only condition for saving us from eternal hell is accepting His gift of salvation and making Him first and foremost in our lives. Even still, we often fail to remember what His Word teaches about priority. **"Blessed are those who hunger and thirst for righteousness, for they shall be satisfied" (Matthew 5:6).**

Nothing convicts me more about idleness in prayer than priority. Of all the excuses I use to justify my indifference, accepting that I fail to make God top priority cuts the deepest. My flesh rails against guilt and shame because I want to point out all the ways I do apply God's Word in my daily actions. I long for Him to give me credit for working a full-time job, cooking meals at home, washing dishes, doing laundry, cleaning the house, mowing the lawn, helping my family, and other tasks. From my perspective, I am trading quality time in prayer for serving my family. What could possibly be wrong with that trade-off?

Serving our families is not all about them, though. Reality testifies that our actions impact us most. For instance, we all need to eat, sleep, and tend to our personal hygiene. These functions have no bearing on whether we have a family. They are independent, survival needs. Regardless, that should not stop us from making them dual-purpose opportunities. For instance, we can lie in bed at night and pray as we fall asleep. While eating breakfast, lunch, or dinner, we can easily pray and thank God for His provision. The same goes for personal hygiene when we are getting ready and have time to quietly think and pray while we multitask.

Speaking to God can happen at any time and in any location. We must simply seize the opportunity and use it to tell Him what is on our hearts and minds. That is the essence of praying without ceasing—leveraging every waking hour towards fellowship with the Lord. That does not mean we substitute quality time with Him only when we feel like it. Rather, it means we intentionally shift God away from being a checklist item we focus on once a day to being the continual, central focus of our entire life.

I once bought the lie that prayer had to be structured and rigid to be effective. I would often wait to talk to God or for my schedule to open up, because I thought I needed a special time and place for prayer. The problem was that I was always too busy, so I cancelled my daily quiet time with Him. Days turned into weeks and months before I realized I had distanced myself from Him altogether. In my mind, prayer had to be all or nothing, not a discipline of talking to God frequently. As a result, I wasted years of my life being isolated from the Lord and it showed in my undisciplined faith journey.

Prayer is not an all or nothing spiritual discipline. It is a combination of reserved time with our heavenly Father and momentary check-ins. We all need wisdom and counsel for decisions we make, so why not talk to God more often? Perhaps if we prioritized prayer throughout the day, we would be less anxious and seek His kingdom first before elevating our own. In the end, we are wise to make God our central focus rather than another legalistic box to check off at the end of the day, because prayer is all about priority.

Application

1. What is one easy adjustment you can make to prioritize prayer?

2. Think about your average day and make a list of all priorities in your life. How long does each function take to complete?

3. Once you have your day planned out, think about how you can leverage that time with dual-purpose. When can you pray more?

4. At a minimum, how can you discipline yourself to pray to God at the beginning and end of your day? What adjustments do you need to make to your schedule, if any?

5. Do you struggle with "all or nothing" prayers? Why or why not?

6. How does your life testify that God is your central focus? What do you regret about the time you have not spent with Him?

7. How can you begin to seek first the kingdom of God and His righteousness? What does that look like moving forward?

Prayer

Lord, Your patience is amazing. Thank You for loving me when I fail to keep You at the forefront of my mind. There are many decisions I make daily, and I rarely choose to seek Your wisdom and counsel as one of them. Please forgive me for placing myself before You. Pride has become a huge issue in my life, hindering me from talking to You throughout my day. I will never understand the true power of prayer until I discipline my heart and mind to make it a priority. Help me prune daily activities from my schedule which are inconsequential so I can make prayer my central focus. You deserve better and I intend to give You the first fruits of my time. Amen.

Day 13 – Insecurity

Excuse: I'm not spiritual enough to pray.

"Finally, be strong in the Lord and in the strength of his might.
Put on the whole armor of God, that you may be able
to stand against the schemes of the devil."

— *Ephesians 6:10–11* —

Who does not deal with a little insecurity these days? It seems commonplace to wonder if we have the strength and might to defend ourselves when trouble comes our way. When it comes to prayer, many of us doubt whether we are spiritual enough to stand before the throne of grace. We feel sinful and unworthy, so we avoid God altogether rather than run to Him in brokenness and repentance. The truth of the matter is that none of us are worthy to stand before the Lord almighty and live to tell about it. We will never be good enough, smart enough, or strong enough apart from Christ, so we must abide in Him at all times.

Assuming we need to reach some pinnacle of righteousness to stand before God is simply false. He does not expect us to cleanse ourselves before bowing to Him in prayer. Quite the opposite! He expects us to cry out in brokenness because we are hopelessly lost and need His mercy. Unfortunately, we often abandon our need to pray because of despair. We feel unworthy because we know the enormity of our sins. We also lament the wake of destruction caused by sins which could have been avoided had we followed the Lord's commands. In other words, prayer can be difficult to reconcile if we assume that only the righteous are worthy to pray, not the sick who desperately need a doctor (Luke 5:31-32).

I believed the lie of insecurity for a dark season of my life. When confronted with the magnitude of my addiction, I avoided confessing my sins to God on countless occasions. He gave me moments of clarity to open my eyes and convict my spirit, but I never took those opportunities to lean into prayer as a means of changing my ways. Rather, I walked away defeated with no hope that tomorrow could be different. I remember thinking, "I'm not spiritual enough to talk to God," so I did not even try. Instead, I accepted defeat and distanced myself. I felt unworthy to stand before Him and confess the same sins time and again. Shame baited me into giving up on prayer and my faith suffered mightily for believing the enemy's lie.

Satan is a master manipulator. He waits patiently for us to isolate ourselves and then seizes upon the opportunity to pick us apart. He wants us to wallow in self-pity and regret our foolish decisions so that we do not even lift our eyes to heaven but rest in our depravity and unworthiness. However, in Romans 3:10–12, Paul reminds us that no one is perfect and we all need salvation. Again, we will never be good enough to warrant the ransom Jesus paid to set us free. The sacrifice He made could never be repaid. Therefore, all we can do is bow before His throne in reverence and humble ourselves before the judgment seat on which He stands.

What is interesting about the excuse, "I'm not spiritual enough," is that it presupposes a standard which is not entirely accurate. Yes, God wants us to humble ourselves daily, but reverence is all about respect, not achievement. The Lord is far more concerned about the posture of our hearts than the list of accomplishments we use to seek His approval and prove our righteousness. Look no further than the parable of the Pharisee and the Tax Collector (Luke 18:9-14) as clear evidence that the Lord desires only a broken spirit, not spiritual achievement.

Another area where Satan preys upon insecurity is the manner in which we pray. We have all been in a room full of spiritually mature Christians who are prayer warriors (or so we think). Their prayers sound eloquent and the words and phrases they use are profound. When we hear such prayers we tend to covet their ability to pray, as well as lament our own struggle of finding the right words to say. However, comparison is one of the tools Satan uses to tempt us to abandon prayer. He makes us think our prayers are shallow and immature, and that God would never accept our feeble attempts to honor Him as He rightly deserves.

We must remember that our enemy knows Scripture better than we do and can twist it enough to make us assume the Lord expects verbal eloquence over heartfelt brokenness. That is the danger of assuming He has any expectation of us other than humility and reverence when we pray. It is easy to fall victim to that lie and wonder why we feel so lonely and defeated, for we forget it is only by grace through faith that we have the opportunity to stand before the Lord and share our hearts freely. By ourselves, we will never be good enough to pray, yet we have access to God's heart because our Savior made a way to cleanse us from all unrighteousness.

When I reflect upon my past, I see a wicked man unworthy to stand before the Lord and live. In hindsight, I should have confessed, **"Woe is me! For I am lost; for I am a man of unclean lips, and I dwell in the midst of a people of unclean lips; for my eyes have seen the King, the LORD of hosts!" (Isaiah 6:5)**. No good in me warrants being called a child of God. Nevertheless, He saved me, not because I deserved an opportunity to prove my worth but because He knew I was lost without Him. I will never be spiritual enough to pray to God, but that is not the point. I am saved by grace. Thus, I am worthy to cast my eyes upon the Lord and live.

Application

1. What does it mean to not be spiritual enough to pray? How have you bought into that lie?

2. How have you fallen victim to insecurity which has hindered your prayer life?

3. How can Ephesians 6:10-11 help you overcome insecurity?

4. What lies has Satan whispered in your ear to tempt you to give up praying to God?

5. Do you believe you are worthy enough to stand before the Lord and live? Why or why not?

6. How have you compared the quality of your prayers to others? What impact has that had on your prayer life?

7. Read Isaiah 6:1-7. Why is reverence so critical to maintaining a healthy discipline of prayer?

Prayer

Lord, You are the author of all creation. I praise You for making Yourself known to me—drawing me out of darkness and into the light of Your grace and mercy. I confess that I have run away from Your presence because of insecurity. For whatever reason, I assume that I need to clean myself up before coming to You. Please forgive me for saying, "I'm not spiritual enough." It is simply an excuse. I have no reason to avoid prayer other than conviction, and I pray that I run to You in genuine repentance, not further away in fear of condemnation. You desire brokenness, Lord, so help me sacrifice my pride at the foot of Your cross each day. Amen.

Day 14 – Affirmation

Remedy: The Lord is near to the brokenhearted.

"When the righteous cry for help, the LORD hears and delivers them out of all their troubles. The LORD is near to the brokenhearted and saves the crushed in spirit."

— *Psalm 34:17–18* —

There is something powerful about knowing God hears us when we cry out to Him. In many ways, one of the greatest longings of our hearts is to be heard. We long to know our thoughts and opinions have value and that, at a minimum, the Lord will listen to us even when others refuse. Many of us struggle with insecurity and feelings of inadequacy before the Lord, knowing that He is holy and we are not. Yet despite our shortcomings, the Lord still pursues a relationship with us and desires to know what we are thinking and feeling, regardless of whether we care to talk.

Oftentimes, those we contact when we need to vent are people who will listen, for we would not waste our time if they did not care about what we had to say. We run to them because they have proven their love and support over time by valuing our thoughts and comforting us when we are struggling. Yet, how many times have we gone to those same people and they were unavailable to counsel us? Perhaps they were out of town, too busy, or unable to respond when we needed them. It is a humble reminder that not everyone will be available at our beckoning call when we need help.

Thankfully, the Lord does not have any difficulty picking up the phone when we call. He does not put us on hold nor do we have to leave a message and wait patiently for Him to call us back. The Lord is always available and listening. Why then do we fail to contact Him first? What is it that holds us back from calling upon the name of Jesus instead of a spouse, friend, or parent? The problem is we want affirmation we can physically touch, and reading God's Word does not have the same immediate impact as receiving a warm hug from a loved one when we are hurting.

That does not mean God cares any less. No amount of love we receive from others can compare to the unending love of Jesus. Reason being, **"Greater love has no one than this, that someone lay down his life for his friends" (John 15:13).** Our Savior willingly suffered and died in our place to secure our eternal salvation. He atoned for every sin we will ever commit (past, present, and future). He did not just take a bullet to save us momentarily. He bled and died to save our souls eternally. How then could the love of man ever compare to God's love for us?

The challenge is we crave instant gratification, and oftentimes prayer fails to quench our thirst the way a loved one can. That is because we often fail to see the Bible as a living and breathing entity (Heb. 4:12). For instance, when we begin to open our eyes and ears to God's Word, the Spirit magnifies truth in our hearts and we begin to hear the Lord's voice. His soft whisper (1 Kings 19:12) can only be perceived when we quiet our minds. That means we must filter out worldly distractions so we are not tempted to give up on prayer altogether. Hearing God's voice is not easy. It requires patience to hear Him calling us home to rest in His presence, but it is incredibly rewarding when we do.

Psalm 34:17-18 is a favorite Scripture passage of mine. It reminds me that when I am struggling to survive, the Lord is never far away. Actually, He is closer to me than a brother and hears me every time I call upon His name. Regardless of the trials I face, He is always by my side. What I often forget, though, is I must be actively pursuing sanctification and allowing Him to shape my character. I must also remember that a righteous man is not perfect but perfectible, which requires me to evaluate my heart's condition and reconcile whether I am moving toward the safety of Jesus or running away from His presence to avoid conviction.

The promise God offers me is that I am safe and sound in His sovereign protection, yet it is my responsibility to determine what happens next. The problem is sometimes I do not want to make a conscious effort to pray and seek His wisdom and counsel. I would rather wallow in self-pity than take hold of the lifeline He provides to save me from calamity. Yet despite my naïve foolishness, God continues to welcome me into His presence each day. He does not condemn me for not speaking to Him in prayer but waits for me to come to my senses and return home broken and repentant.

What an incredible picture of unconditional love! When we are struggling with insecurity and the enemy is baiting us to believe we will never be good enough, we can rest assured that God will never forsake us. As the Psalmist declares, the Lord hears and delivers us from the hands of the enemy because He is always by our side, promising salvation to those who trust in the name of Jesus. With such a powerful declaration of hope and security, why would we ever pass up the opportunity to commune with the Lord in prayer?

When we call upon Jesus' holy name, we acknowledge that we are powerless to overcome the forces of darkness on our own. We desperately need the Holy Spirit to guide us unto righteousness and that begins with surrendering our insecurities and self-doubt at the foot of the cross. God longs to heal our broken hearts, but we must make the first step and cry out to Him alone for salvation. Only then will we find rest for our weary souls.

Application

1. Do you believe God hears you when you call upon His name for help? Why or why not?

2. When you are struggling, who do you typically contact to vent your frustrations and seek wise counsel? Why?

3. When you need wisdom and discernment, why should the Lord be your first point of contact rather than a loved one?

4. How can desiring instant gratification hinder your prayer life?

5. Why is Psalm 34:17-18 such a powerful encouragement? What reassurance does it provide that you need to remember?

6. As in the Parable of the Prodigal Son, why does God not chase after you but instead, waits patiently for you to come home?

7. How can your prayer life be transformed knowing God is near to the brokenhearted and saves the crushed in spirit?

Prayer

Lord, I praise You for being my rock and my salvation, a fortress of protection in my hour of need. I do not warrant the patience You continuously show me, but I humbly thank You for Your unending grace and mercy when I need refuge. There seems to be no shortage of trials I face each day, but I know that You are always by my side. Help me run to the shelter of Your wings when I am tired and weary from spiritual warfare. I often cry out to You as a last resort rather than my first inclination. Please forgive me. You have been faithful to me in ways I cannot fully comprehend. Help me to never forget that hope and healing are found in You alone. Amen.

Day 15 – Distractions

Excuse: I can't focus my mind to pray.

"If then you have been raised with Christ, seek the things that are above, where Christ is, seated at the right hand of God. Set your minds on things that are above, not on things that are on earth."

— *Colossians 3:1–2* —

How many times have we started to pray and suddenly been distracted? There are numerous reasons why we could easily get sidetracked, but there is a level of frustration which comes with distractions that overwhelms our minds with defeat. If we take time out of our day to pray, why do we give up so easily when our minds drift from one thing to the next? We made the effort to pray, so why do we allow frustration to wage war upon our psyche and tempt us to throw in the towel on quality time with God?

I admit that this excuse in particular is one I wrestle with daily. I get so aggravated because I cannot seem to focus my attention and pray effectively. My anger stems from the fact that I genuinely desire a healthy prayer life. I do not want to just go through the motions. Rather, I want to offer God a pleasing sacrifice which means I will clear my mind of distractions to hear His voice. However, it seems every time I begin praying about one thing, my mind pinballs in a different direction and I find myself miles apart from where I began, which irritates me to no end.

Within seconds of recalibrating my direction, I feel defeated for losing focus and abruptly stopping my prayer. With little persuasion, Satan can get me self-funneling and distracted. What I often fail to realize is that God is not as concerned about my mind drifting as I am. He already knows my thoughts and feelings before I speak, so He is not offended by my lack of focus. He is pleased that I am prioritizing a discipline of prayer. What He is more concerned about is my relenting spirit which often gives in to the devil's schemes and accepts defeat by giving up.

Even though we may suffer from pinball tendencies in prayer, it does not necessarily mean our efforts are in vain. Satan would have us believe that if we cannot focus our minds, we might as well give up trying. Consequently, we believe a lie more than we care to admit. Why? What makes us think God would ever declare to us, **"I never knew you; depart from me, you workers of lawlessness" (Matthew 7:23)**? That judgment is reserved for those who do the bidding of Satan, not those working out their salvation with fear and trembling before the Lord (Phil. 2:12).

Nevertheless, we often think that if we are distracted, God does not hear us because we expect Him to respond like we do. For instance, if our children begin to tell us a story and tangent off on something completely different, how long does it take before we say something to get them back on track? Perhaps we tune them out and stop listening. Both scenarios are possible depending upon our mood. But just because we might act that way, there is nothing in Scripture which warns us that God behaves similarly.

Actually, Scripture affirms that the Lord is long-suffering and will provide us ample opportunity to wake up and refocus our attention on Him. **"The Lord is not slow to fulfill his promise as some count slowness, but is patient toward you, not wishing that any should perish, but that all should reach repentance" (2 Peter 3:9)**. God's patience is an attribute of His character which we cannot put a price tag on. He endures the wages of sin every time we yield to temptation and disobey His Word. Truly, we drive nails deeper into the hands and feet of Jesus when we sin, yet He would pay our debt and do it all over again if it meant we would humble ourselves and embrace genuine repentance.

Sacrificial love is indescribable. Our minds cannot comprehend devotion of that magnitude. Why then would we ever imagine God walking away or tuning us out when our minds begin to drift in prayer? It is beneficial for us to work on focusing our attention better, but by no means is God so angry by our pinball tendencies to justify us giving up. Throwing in the towel is more about quitting on ourselves than the Lord abandoning us. Therefore, an attitude adjustment is required if we intend to push past Satan's lies and continue praying, even when our minds begin to drift off course from where we began.

Writing this devotional has caused a rollercoaster of emotions within me. As stated previously, I struggle mightily with prayer, and being easily distracted has become a bottleneck in my faith journey. However, as I have purged my thoughts and feelings, God's Word has spoken to my heart. I am overwhelmed by the love of my Savior who is infinitely bigger than my insecurities. Now, my biggest regret is that I allowed the enemy to twist my understanding of God's love and draw me away from quality time in prayer for so long.

I am a work-in-progress, though, and learn more each day about what a gift it is to pray to God directly. I have no doubt that distractions will continue to be a source of frustration in my life, but I believe God does not feel the same disdain toward me as I do when I yield to disruptions. I trust He is pleased when I fight my fleshly tendencies to serve myself and refocus my mind to hear His voice speaking. Distractions could easily be an excuse for me to give up on prayer, but I continue to press on knowing my Savior will never forsake me despite my wayward heart and drifting mind.

Application

1. Do you struggle fighting pinball tendencies in prayer? Why or why not?

2. How have you allowed frustration with distractions to cut your prayers short? Why do you allow them to continue?

3. Do you believe God hears your prayers when your mind begins to drift off course on a tangent?

4. Which outside distractions (kids, job, extracurriculars, busyness, etc.) hinder you from praying more?

5. Which internal distractions (frustration, anger, disappointment, etc.) cut your prayers short before they begin?

6. Why is 2 Peter 3:9 such a powerful encouragement for a healthy prayer life, regardless of distractions?

7. What attitude adjustment do you need to make to not allow the enemy to bait you into feeling defeated by distractions?

Prayer

Lord, You know that I long to spend quality time with You. Yet despite my efforts, I feel as if I cannot gain traction in prayer because of spiritual warfare. Why I allow Satan to toy with my mind makes no sense. Your Word is clear. You have never forsaken me and You never will. Why then do I assume my prayers are in vain? Help me filter out the enemy's lies and continue talking to You, regardless of whether my mind pinballs in countless directions. Most of all, thank You for Your Spirit interceding on my behalf and making clear to You what I fail to adequately convey in my prayers. Amen.

Day 16 – Intentionality

Remedy: Ponder the path of your feet.

"Let your eyes look directly forward, and your gaze be straight before you. Ponder the path of your feet; then all your ways will be sure. Do not swerve to the right or to the left; turn your foot away from evil."

— Proverbs 4:25–27 —

Sometimes, it feels like prayer should be easy, but oftentimes it is not. No matter how hard we concentrate, our minds tend to veer off course despite our best intent to remain connected to God. What we need is focus and determination, but intentionality is the linchpin which holds it all together. Purposeful intent is all about aligning our thoughts, beliefs, hopes, and desires into one singular direction. It requires that we focus clearly on an objective with firm determination to reach our goal. Nevertheless, success or failure is dependent on what is driving our mission, not wishful thinking.

Implementing spiritual disciplines requires steadfast, deliberate focus. We can wish all day long for positive change to occur, but without determination to reach our end goals, we are destined to fail miserably. Yet, how many of us sit back and expect change to take place without making any effort whatsoever? If we are being completely honest, we tend to wait for God to do all the work and grant our wishes. Only if we are in crisis mode do we increase our prayer efforts until God meets our needs, to which then we default back to expecting heart change with little to no effort on our part.

It is humbling to admit, but I am guilty of complaining about my prayer life far too often. Reason being, I do not want to accept that the reason my discipline is practically non-existent is because I fail to intentionally make God a priority. As a Christian, it is embarrassing to look back upon the years I wasted and recognize how foolish I was to complain. I was unwilling to discipline myself and change the error of my ways. No wonder prayer has been such a struggle! I expected intimacy with God to develop without communicating on a daily basis with Him.

Similarly, my marriage would be in dire straits if I did not make intentionality a priority. My wife would feel forgotten, abused, and unappreciated if I disregarded her feelings but expected her to meet my needs daily. Why then do I struggle connecting the dots between my lack of effort and subsequent poor attitude concerning prayer? Perhaps I am delusional to believe I am a man after God's own heart without prayer as my spiritual anchor. The entire book of Psalms proves that prayer was an integral part of David's life. He spoke to God honestly and frequently, and the Lord blessed Him despite his many faults and foolish decisions. Why then can I not do the same?

Our biggest problem with intentionality is it magnifies how much we desire an intimate relationship with the Lord. It eliminates the lip-service aspect of our faith and forces us to put our money where our mouth is. We cannot hide from the fact that a healthy prayer life is contingent upon carving out time for God in our daily schedules. We must make a concerted effort. If not, we have no justification for complaining about how numb we feel praying. Intentionality is a black or white issue we would rather ignore because it is convicting. Nevertheless, we cannot hope for a brighter tomorrow without seriously making changes today.

Proverbs 4:25-27 offers an easy recipe for us to follow and draw closer to the Lord. All we are expected to do is look straightforward, keep our eyes fixed upon Jesus, and deliberately carve out time for Him. As a result, we must wisely consider our ways, because God does not want us to be consumed by the things of this world which distract us from quality time in prayer. Rather, He wants us to make a deliberate effort to walk by faith and not worry about things we could be doing instead.

If you are like me, you likely spend too much time thinking about the things you failed to finish today which are waiting for you tomorrow. Lying in bed at night is when I struggle shutting off my brain. Like a supercomputer, I process a ridiculous amount of information and get stressed determining how I will accomplish it all. Only as a last resort do I waive the white flag of surrender and pray to God after exhausting my mind for hours. It is a never-ending cycle of running aimlessly on a hamster's wheel. However, I do not have to keep running in place. I can step off the treadmill of self-dependance and rely upon God instead.

To gain self-control over intentionality, we must realize that we can change direction and begin anew. Just because we have been enslaved to distractions does not mean we are destined to remain there eternally. We can make God our top priority, but we cannot expect Him to do all the work. To successfully discipline ourselves and pray more often, we must keep our eyes transfixed on why we are prioritizing prayer in the first place. For it is one thing to recognize a need for prayer but another to put a strategic plan of action into place to accomplish our goal.

Far too many well-intentioned Christians have hit an emotional wall because they feel nothing. It is not surprising considering those of us who complain about prayer are banging our heads against the wall in frustration, unwilling to do much else to shift our perspective and change our ways. Nonetheless, if we truly understood why we needed to pray, taking necessary steps to remedy our issues would not feel so daunting but realistically achievable.

Application

1. Why is intentionality so convicting to your prayer life?

2. Is your communication with God one-directional? If yes, why? If no, what steps have you taken to maintain open dialogue?

3. Consider a season of your life when God made Himself known to you. What did your prayer life look like at the time?

4. Is it possible to have a vibrant relationship with God without praying to Him and reading His Word daily? Why or why not?

5. Which directional aspect of Proverbs 4:25-27 do you struggle applying to prayer? How so?

6. How can you stop worrying about tomorrow and refocus your mind to pray instead?

7. How have you hit a wall spiritually? What is one change you can make to start tomorrow off on a new path with God?

Prayer

Lord, I am lazy. I hate admitting that. Yet, when push comes to shove, I expect You to do all the work to maintain our relationship. Please forgive me. I have no one to blame but myself for feeling parched and empty inside when You patiently wait for me to come to my senses and return home. It is difficult to recognize how much of a prodigal I truly am. I cannot hide how I want You to give me everything I desire with no expectations in return. I know that You encourage me to make a conscious effort, yet I fail terribly. Please help me begin anew by intentionally setting aside time each day to read Your Word, humble myself, and pray earnestly. Amen.

Day 17 – Procrastination
Excuse: I will just pray later.

"The sluggard does not plow in the autumn;
he will seek at harvest and have nothing."

— *Proverbs 20:4* —

Time is a precious commodity. We all have the same 24-hours to pick and choose how we will spend our day. We can live for ourselves and the demands of this world or choose to follow Christ. Therefore, intentionality is paramount to ensure we are focusing our time and attention developing a deeper relationship with God through prayer. In many ways, tomorrow is a fresh opportunity for positive change to occur. It allows us the opportunity to abandon our selfish ways and draw closer to the Lord. All we must do is prioritize prayer and take the necessary measures to carve out time with God in our daily schedules.

Temptation abounds because Satan will use the hope of tomorrow to convince us that we have all the time in the world to change. In theory, it seems like we do, which is why it is relatively easy to put off what we could accomplish today because of physical exhaustion, mental fatigue, or emotional weariness. Sometimes, we just need to unplug from our never-ending checklists and relax. Yet in the same token, if we are not careful, we can easily forget why we rested in the first place and never utilize the opportunity to cast our cares upon the Lord. Consequently, procrastination is a dangerous excuse we must take seriously because the enemy knows we will forever be stuck in neutral if we foolishly assume that tomorrow is nothing but 100% guaranteed.

Scripture warns, **"Do not boast about tomorrow, for you do not know what a day may bring" (Proverbs 27:1).** The biggest mistake we could make is assuming we will live to see another day. As a man who almost died of a heart attack at age 44, I can testify that life is fragile indeed. Moreover, as a father of a college student who now lives away from home for the majority of the year, I am reminded that my window of opportunity to teach my eldest how to pray is long gone. She already graduated from high school, and I have nothing but regret for putting off what I should have taught her while she was still living at home.

That is not to say I cannot begin anew and find creative ways to pray with her more from a distance. God can restore what is lost and make all things new if I am committed to right the wrongs I made throughout her life. However, I must be intentional and stop procrastinating my spiritual leadership. My daughter is always open to heeding my advice and hearing what I have to say, but now is the time to model prayer, not put it off for a later date. It is easy to punt leadership responsibilities to my wife or make empty promises to improve, but who am I fooling other than myself? My track record proves how poorly I have modeled prayer in our home. I was lazy and disinterested, and that inevitably led to constant procrastination.

The key to lasting change is remembering that tomorrow is not guaranteed. Yes, it sounds cliché but is painfully true. Anyone who has lost a loved one unexpectedly can empathize with the pain of regret and not taking full advantage of quality time. The challenge is we fail to appreciate what we have until it is lost or taken away, and time is arguably the most precious asset we have at our disposal. For instance, those who have procrastinated a decision to follow Christ can agree that time wasted can never be recovered. How then do we avoid falling into a similar trap?

Positive change begins and ends with understanding why time is so very precious. We will never follow through on putting a plan of action into place if we do not understand why we are changing in the first place. It seems like a foregone conclusion, but the factors motivating our personal change will determine if we pass the test or fail miserably. For example, if I am doing daily devotions with my girls simply because my wife pressed me to do it, I will likely drift away from being consistent because I am only going through the motions to appease her request and quench any nagging. In turn, motivation must have a sense of urgency to grasp the big picture if I expect positive change to stand the test of time.

Oftentimes, we fail to see the forest through the trees of our faith journey. We misunderstand the importance of spiritual disciplines because we believe they exist in a bubble. Unfortunately, our ability to carve out time daily for prayer and Bible study impacts far more than ourselves. It influences our marriages, homes, workplaces, and communities. Being intentional to grow spiritually overflows into the lives of those we interact with daily. To assume otherwise is nonsense, because others are blessed when God has ample opportunity to mold and shape our personal character.

In the end, procrastination is nothing more than an empty excuse to pacify God and others into believing we will follow through on good intentions. Still, even the best laid plans are meaningless if we never make a conscious effort to remedy the problem. God is long-suffering and immeasurably patient, so we are only fooling ourselves if we put off for tomorrow what can be resolved today. It all comes down to taking full advantage of the time we have been given and investing in our spiritual growth. Tomorrow is not guaranteed. Therefore, we should make the most of today, commit to change, and pray without ceasing before it's too late.

Application

1. What impact has procrastination had on your prayer life?

2. What are the greatest dangers of procrastination? Why is it such a serious excuse to guard against in spiritual disciplines?

3. How has Satan used the hope of tomorrow against you? How have you fallen for his deception?

4. Which regrets you hold to this day are a direct result of laziness? How so?

5. Do you live as if tomorrow is guaranteed? Why or why not?

6. Why is it easy to procrastinate spending quality time with God? How have your spiritual disciplines suffered as a result?

7. How has your procrastination impacted the spiritual disciplines of your family?

Prayer

Lord, I know that tomorrow is not guaranteed, but I often live my life as if I can wait indefinitely to spend quality time with You and not reap the consequences of my actions. I assume I can postpone developing spiritual disciplines when the time is right or more convenient. The challenge is that tomorrow can provide false hope if I am not careful. Satan knows if he can get me to put off prayer and Bible study for just another day, I will never achieve consistency in my faith journey. Please forgive me for allowing him to influence my behavior so easily. I repent of my procrastination and commit to make the necessary changes to prioritize quality time with You without interruption. Amen.

Day 18 – Discipline

Remedy: I train my body and keep it under control.

"Every athlete exercises self-control in all things.
They do it to receive a perishable wreath, but we an imperishable.
So I do not run aimlessly; I do not box as one beating the air.
But I discipline my body and keep it under control, lest after
preaching to others I myself should be disqualified."

— *1 Corinthians 9:25–27* —

Discipline is a touchy subject for most people. We either love it or hate it. It all depends on perspective and the point in time we find ourselves. If we look in the rear-view mirror, we can see how far we have come and the role discipline played in helping us achieve our goals. It can be the reason we fail too. In the moment, discipline is painful because we are being stretched. We would rather avoid it if we could, but that is not how discipline works. Therefore, if we want to develop a healthy prayer life, we must discipline our hearts and minds to do whatever is necessary to create a new normal and stick to the plan.

Discipline is one of those "tough pill to swallow" issues which exposes hypocrisy. For instance, I am a man who prefers structure. I am disciplined to be on time and not late for appointments. I am disciplined taking my heart medications to ensure nothing remotely catastrophic happens to my health. I am disciplined helping around the house each day to cook meals, clean, help with the kids, etc. I am even disciplined making my wife coffee each morning as a way of loving and serving her. By all accounts, I am a very disciplined man, practically-speaking.

Yet, when it comes to prayer, I am as undisciplined as they come. My excuses are many. Ironically, I am far more disciplined making excuses for my lack of spiritual leadership in prayer (outside of praying before a meal) than being a godly role model to my wife and daughters. It is incredibly humbling to look in the mirror and admit failure as a spiritual leader, but I have no one to blame but myself for the lack of fervent prayer in our home. I chose to put other things before God and yield to insecurities. I made excuses rather than doing something about them. Truly, the buck stops with me because it is my sin to bear.

Discipline is a mental battle. Success is defined by putting mind over matter and pushing through pain and discomfort. For example, marathon runners know what it is like to hit a wall when their tank is empty. In the moment, going any further seems impossible. Their bodies are gassed, and giving up seems like a foregone conclusion. However, something happens when runners hit a wall. Somehow, someway, they manage to push through the pain and grind their way to the finish line. They lean upon their physical training discipline instead of focusing on pain and discomfort which compels them to consider quitting entirely.

The same concept applies to prayer. When our bodies are tired and our minds exhausted, we often do not want to stop and pray. We would rather sleep, unplug, or decompress. In many ways, prayer feels like the most illogical decision imaginable when we struggle focusing our minds for just a few minutes. That is what Satan wants us to believe, though. He wants us to look in the mirror and beat ourselves up with guilt and shame for not maintaining discipline in prayer. For even though we might be saved, he is poised to use our identity in Christ against us by overwhelming our minds with regret for the good things we fail to do (Rom. 7:19).

If we call ourselves Christians, prayer should be an integral part of our lives. However, many of us struggle disciplining ourselves to pray daily and the enemy knows it. He uses our faith against us by magnifying our unworthiness in a self-deprecating way. Satan wants us to feel defeated for not spending time with God—to beat ourselves up rather than being led into temptation. It is a brilliant strategy of attack because he has baited more Christians to throw in the towel on prayer due to guilt than anything else. All he has to do is put a spotlight on our lack of discipline and hypocrisy takes center stage, condemning us for not making Jesus top priority.

Let us be clear, though. Discipline is a choice and we are masters of our own domain. We can train ourselves to pray daily or give up entirely. What is more critical is that we maintain proper perspective while building spiritual discipline. For example, if a man is training for a marathon, he does not begin by running 26.2-miles on day #1. He starts out slowly and gradually increases his distance and pace over the span of days, weeks, and months before reaching his goal. Discipline takes time. Why then do we expect to be proficient at prayer if we are at ground zero in our training? Rome was not built in a day and neither will our spiritual disciplines be if we do not take a step back and gain proper perspective.

Success or failure in the art of discipline is all about consistency, intentionality, and determination. All other aspects of prayer will come in due time, but we must have a firm plan of attack to build a healthy discipline of prayer in our lives. God does not expect us to reach the mountaintop overnight. He simply wants us to progress each day toward our summit and push through the pain as we train ourselves to be consistent in our efforts. All we must do is start slowly and build momentum as we set our eyes on growing closer to our Lord and Savior, Jesus Christ.

Application

1. Would you consider yourself disciplined? Why or why not?

2. Why are consistency, intentionality, and determination vital to developing a healthy prayer life?

3. What role does pain and discomfort play in the journey toward discipline? How do they help you appreciate the sacrifices made to achieve your goals?

4. Think of a time when you were running the Christian race and hit a wall spiritually. What did God teach you in that moment?

5. Why does the enemy not want you to be spiritually disciplined?

6. How has Satan held you captive to regret for spiritual disciplines you have failed to accomplish?

7. Spiritually-speaking, why do you believe you can run a marathon when you have never trained to walk a mile?

Prayer

Lord, Your patience with me is greatly appreciated. Despite my best intentions, I struggle from a lack of spiritual discipline in prayer which has hindered my relationship with You. The enemy has me so focused on guilt and shame that I beat myself up rather than take necessary measures to make positive change occur. Please give me wisdom to see my sins clearly and make amends for damages caused due to a lack of spiritual leadership. I cannot model for others what I fail to maintain consistently in my own faith journey. Do whatever it takes to humble me, Lord, so that I prioritize quality time with You above all else. Amen.

Day 19 – Shamefulness
Excuse: I am too sinful to pray.

"I sought the Lord, and he answered me and delivered me from all my fears. Those who look to him are radiant, and their faces shall never be ashamed."

— Psalm 34:4–5 —

No matter how far removed we are from the memories of our past, we cannot escape how wretched we once were apart from Jesus. If we could go back and change things, we would gladly avoid the pain and heartache we brought upon ourselves and others. For better or worse, our former selves are a part of who we are now, but that does not mean we must live as if we are shackled by guilt, shame, and regret. The Lord does not expect us to come into His presence perfected by good works which testify to how we saved ourselves. He knows we are incapable of cleaning up our act which is why He gave us His Spirit to lead us towards righteousness.

The enemy constantly reminds me of how sinful I was and how I continue to fall short of God's perfect standard. Granted, my sins look different than years ago, but the same root of selfishness exists between the two. No matter how hard I try, I will never be good enough to stand justified before the Lord on judgment day because I need salvation through Jesus. I know it and the enemy does as well. In fact, Satan is so intimately aware of my sins that he uses them against me by tempting me to wallow in despair and believe I am nothing more than a lost cause.

In many ways, the excuse, "I am too sinful to pray," is hard to resist believing. It proves how much we hold onto the past even though God promises to forgive those who genuinely repent of their sins. Scripture declares, **"I, I am he who blots out your transgressions for my own sake, and I will not remember your sins" (Isaiah 43:25).** In other words, God does not hold onto the memory of sins or act as if they did not occur. He knows they did. He simply chose to punish Jesus on our behalf rather than hold us ultimately accountable on judgment day.

As a result, shame plays no role in God's master plan to save us from our transgressions. It is merely a weapon of the enemy to keep us shackled to guilt and regret so we give up believing the Gospel. That does not mean God cannot use what the enemy meant for evil to draw us into His presence where hope and healing are found. He does! But if we believe we are too wretched to lift our eyes to the Lord and cry out to Him in prayer, then Satan has already won the battle in our minds. God does not wish to sentence us to hell, which is why He sent Jesus to help us recognize our depravity and repent of our transgressions.

I can attest to wearing the scarlet letter of shame for far too long. I was ashamed to cry out to God in prayer because I felt unworthy to receive His grace and forgiveness. What I came to realize was that shamefulness was a root of selfish pride in my heart. I assumed I was being holy and righteous by beating myself up for past sins. What it actually demonstrated was my lack of faith in Scripture which testified that God cast the memory of my sins from His presence. Therefore, I was the one holding onto guilt, shame, and regret, not God. I could not completely forgive myself, so I made it out as if He was the problem, not me.

The biggest issue with shame is that it plunges us into a state of hopelessness and despair. When we yield to shame, we turn our back on the one who died to free us from sin's bondage. Whether we realize it or not, we are essentially declaring, "God, You are not powerful enough to overcome my shame!" Most likely, none of us believe that, but actions speak louder than words when we throw in the towel on prayer and believe that our sins are too great for Him to overcome. God is always present and listening to our cries. He waits patiently for us to relinquish our fears and lay our shame at the foot of the cross where it truly belongs.

For many, our prayer lives are at a complete standstill. We cannot fathom that God would accept wretched sinners like us who profess saving faith in Jesus yet yield to temptation. It seems illogical that God would continually forgive us and provide infinite opportunities to go and sin no more (John 8:11). Even so, the Lord is faithful when we are adulterous and loves us in ways we will never fully comprehend. Believing the excuse, "I am too sinful to pray," is naïve and foolish. Nowhere in Scripture does it say that God could care less about the brokenhearted. Quite the opposite! He is closer to us in our time of need than we realize. We just need to surrender our shame to Him once and for all.

As a former liar, manipulator, blasphemer, and hypocrite, I am fully aware of my unworthiness to stand justified before the throne of grace. My mind cannot comprehend why Jesus died for my sins. I do not deserve such a priceless gift as salvation, yet God made a way for me to spend eternity with Him through the blood of His Son. Considering how immeasurable God's love truly is, how could I ever allow the enemy to hold me captive to shame when I have repented of my sins? Why would I give Satan the opportunity to make me believe I will forever be enslaved to guilt and regret? I am unworthy to stand before God's throne forgiven and redeemed, but God still made a way. Therefore, I will praise Him all the more because He paid the ultimate sacrifice to set me free.

Application

1. What role has shame played in your past and present life?

2. How has Satan enslaved your mind to guilt, shame, and regret?

3. Which aspect of your past do you wish you could change? Why?

4. What is the common denominator between the sins of your past and present? What do they have in common?

5. How strongly do you believe Isaiah 43:25? What impact can it have overcoming shamefulness through prayer?

6. How can having a sense of unworthiness lead to selfish pride?

7. Why must you never allow shame to devolve into hopelessness and despair? Which dangers should you avoid?

8. Knowing you will continue to make foolish decisions and sin against the Lord, how can you guard against shame?

Prayer

Lord, it goes without saying that I am a wretched sinner, yet You willingly died for me. I will never understand why You would send Your Son to suffer in my place. I do not deserve such a selfless act of pure love. Instead, I warrant wrath and punishment for my sins. Heaven knows the enemy reminds me daily of how wretched I am. He taunts me with shame and tempts me to identify myself by the scarlet letter of past sins instead of Jesus' blood. Help me to never allow his voice to overpower Yours. Remind me through Your holy Word of who I am in Christ—purchased and redeemed by the lamb of God. Thank You for saving me, Lord. I will forever praise Your name for saving a wretch like me. Amen.

Day 20 – Reverence

Remedy: Woe is me, for I am lost.

*"And I said: 'Woe is me! For I am lost; for I am a man
of unclean lips, and I dwell in the midst of a people of unclean lips;
for my eyes have seen the King, the LORD of hosts!'"*

— Isaiah 6:5 —

The scarlet letter of shame is a challenge for most Christians to reconcile, because it magnifies how unworthy we are to stand before the throne of grace and receive pardon for our sins. King David acknowledged how difficult it was for him to overcome guilt and shame when reflecting upon the enormity of his sins against the Lord. **"For I know my transgressions, and my sin is ever before me. Against you, you only, have I sinned and done what is evil in your sight, so that you may be justified in your words and blameless in your judgment" (Psalm 51:3–4).**

David understood the grave consequences of sin. The child he bore in his adultery with Bathsheba did not live because the Lord intervened. Death had become a common theme in David's life and the shame associated with having Bathsheba's husband killed only compounded the wake of destruction he caused. Nevertheless, what we read in Psalm 51 is not self-pity but self-recognition of his soul's depravity apart from God. David embraced repentance and atoned for his sins, but it was his posture of reverence before the Lord that allowed him to cast off the scarlet letter he carried.

If we research shame in the dictionary, we will discover that pride creates the ideal environment for sin to flourish. Scripture teaches, **"Pride goes before destruction, and a haughty spirit before a** fall" **(Proverbs 16:18)**. Pride is not a remedy used to defeat shame but its root cause. As a result, if we desire to overcome feelings of true unworthiness, we must mirror the posture of Isaiah who modeled reverence and respect before the Lord.

I have always been enamored with Isaiah's vision because it not only conveys the glory of God, which is indescribable, but magnifies the stark contrast between holiness and sin. When Isaiah gazed upon the majesty of God, he was overwhelmed. God's glory filled the room and he quickly recognized his wretchedness before the Lord of hosts. Guilt, shame, and regret overwhelmed his heart and mind. He did not need a reminder of how far he had fallen from grace. Grief over sin immediately entered his mind, evidenced by how he responded to the vision.

Reverence is not the antidote to shame we often envision. It feels old-fashioned, archaic, and religious—not surprising considering how respect for eldership and authority is waning in our culture today. We have forgotten what it means to fear the Lord because our knowledge and understanding of Scripture is minimal at best. We spend little time reading the Bible and developing perspective and discernment in our lives. Thus, it should come as no surprise when we struggle mightily with prayer. We find no real purpose or reason to read His Word based on our behavior. Why then would we waste our time talking to Him in prayer as well?

In many ways, pride and shame are a dysfunctional package deal. Indeed, pride goes before destruction, but it often hinders us from breaking away from shame as well. For this reason, reverence is such a powerful tool to lean on when the enemy overwhelms our minds with guilt. It reminds us of our depravity but more so that God is powerful and can wash away our iniquities if we own our sins and repent of our transgressions. In other words, it means we respect the judgment seat of Christ and what inevitably awaits us if we do not fear His ability to cast us into hell for eternity.

Reverence is the true key which unlocks the door to everlasting freedom in Christ. For without revering who Jesus is as the Son of God, we will never see a necessity for repentance in our lives and act upon our need for reconciliation. Without respecting the Spirit's conviction, we will also never turn away from sin and temptation to choose salvation through Christ. And without heartfelt worship for our Almighty Creator, we will never know what it feels like to be welcomed home by our Father in heaven who loves us so much that He sacrificed His Son in our place.

Reverence of the trinity is not merely obedience but a willful act of submission and surrender to God's supreme authority. My life would not be what it is today without humbly bowing in reverence before the Lord. I am never far removed from the memory of my sins because, like David, they are always before me. I cannot take back the wake of destruction I caused others nor forget how my sins nailed Jesus to the cross. Those are the consequences of my selfish actions, but they do not define me either. Yes, I am a sinner in the hands of a holy God, but I am cleansed by the blood of the Lamb who died to set me free.

That is the Good News of the Gospel and the reason we can stand boldly before the throne of grace, purified of all unrighteousness. Shame is a destructive tool used by Satan to keep us enslaved to the memory of past sins. However, reverence magnifies humility in our hearts and compels us to bow our knees at the feet of Jesus in thankfulness for what He has done. That does not mean we will avoid giving an account for our lives on judgment day. Rather, it reassures us that we will be acquitted of our crimes because Jesus died to save our souls from eternal separation with the Father.

Application

1. How would you define reverence? Why should it be an essential part of your daily prayer life?

2. Do you relate to King David's admission in Psalm 51:3-4? Why or why not?

3. How can you break away from the bondage of guilt and shame if your past sins are always top of mind?

4. What sticks out about Isaiah's reverent posture before the Lord? What can you learn from his example?

5. What does reverence teach about having respect for authority?

6. Why should you revere Jesus as Lord and Savior? What makes Him worthy of honor and glory?

7. Why is reverence such a powerful accountability tool to keep you humble before the Lord?

Prayer

Lord, I am reminded that even if I do not praise You, the rocks will cry out and glorify Your name. You certainly do not need my adoration and affection, but I give them freely because You have done exceedingly more than I could ask for or imagine. You died in my place and I cannot repay that debt no matter how hard I try. It is a priceless gift which deserves devotion and respect. Help me to never forget Your loving sacrifice. I bow in reverence and humility before Your throne because You are worthy. I no longer need to live in shame because Your blood set me free. As such, help me to never forget how amazing Your grace is to my weary soul. Amen.

Day 21 – Cynicism

Excuse: Prayer won't help my situation.

"The fool says in his heart, 'There is no God.' They are corrupt,
they do abominable deeds; there is none who does good."

— *Psalm 14:1* —

How often do we examine our lives from a glass-half-empty perspective? What causes us to have a cynical attitude when things are actually glass-half-full and trending positively? The truth of the matter is we all struggle with a poor attitude at times and look at things from a negative lens. Sometimes, life throws us a curveball we do not expect or takes a sharp turn in a direction which leads to nowhere in particular. That does not mean God lacks a divine plan or purpose for the hardships we face. It simply means we need to lean harder into prayer and allow Him ample opportunity to reveal His will for our lives in due time.

Cynicism is like a disease. It can spread easily to others if we are not careful. The more we look for a black cloud in any situation, the more we cast a dark shadow on the attitude and temperament of others as well. Nowhere is this more evident than at home where our family hears our blunt, honest, and unfiltered opinions. We tend to take their forgiveness for granted when we vent our frustrations because we use them as a sounding board. The problem is we are far less concerned with how our cynicism comes across because we are self-focused. From our perspective, we just need to get things off our chest and vent our feelings. Unfortunately, what others see and hear is a lack of faith in God who is powerful enough to overcome our negative attitudes.

Assuming that prayer will never help us escape the chains of pessimism is foolish. God has clearly demonstrated that He will answer our cries for help so long as we take our hand off the wheel and allow Him to take control. **"If my people who are called by my name humble themselves and pray and seek my face and turn from their wicked ways, then I will hear from heaven and will forgive their sin and heal their land" (2 Chronicles 7:14)**. As such, Jesus is not only Savior but Lord of our lives. We relinquish control to Him because He sees what we cannot and knows what lies on the other side of the horizon.

Letting go is not easy, though. I allowed cynicism to cloud my judgment and hinder me from seeking the Lord's wisdom on many occasions. My self-reliant attitude put a wall up between God and I. Foolishly, I did not believe prayer could help my situation, so I failed to make the effort. Looking back, I believed that life would happen as God willed, regardless of whether I prayed or not. However, I merely used God's sovereignty as a cover or smokescreen to justify my lack of prayer. Cynicism gave way to doubt, and I found myself avoiding prayer altogether because I did not believe it could change my situation for the better.

I had placed expectations on God to answer how I felt was best. If He did not answer in the time or manner of my choosing, I had all the more reason to give up trying and remain cynical. I was not looking to change my ways but fishing for a reason to sidestep my lack of faith in the power of prayer. What I failed to realize was that my family noticed when I wallowed in negativity and voiced my raw and unfiltered opinions. They knew whether I prayed for God's wisdom or not. They saw me when I was living independent from the Lord and leaning on my own understanding rather than relying upon His strength in my hour of need.

Keep in mind, it is one thing to believe prayer will not help our situation but another to say it out loud. Being so bold as to declare that quality time with God is void of value is a declaration of distrust and unbelief in the almighty Creator of the universe. It is tough because none of us want to admit that cynicism actually poisons our relationship with God. We would rather say we are having a bad day or insinuate that our negativity is an exception to the rule rather than a common occurrence. The last thing we want to own is our doubt of God's omniscient sovereignty, but it is inevitably what we must reconcile in our hearts because it is true.

When I think back on the worst sins of my past, cynicism is front and center. My addiction to pornography is a prime example. I can remember praying to God, "Take this desire away from me!" but I lacked faith to believe it was possible. Far in the background, doubt clouded my judgment in God's ability to answer my prayers. Despite my desire to straighten up and fly right, I remained enslaved to my flesh. I could not understand why I failed to earn victory over my sins, so I gave up trying. I did not see the results I hoped for, so I stopped praying. It seemed evident that prayer was not helping my situation, and in my mind, I had no reason to continue.

What I learned was that God would not answer the desires of my heart if I did not believe He was able to make all things new. In one respect, I made the effort to pray, but I also held close to disbelief because I expected Him to miraculously remove my fleshly desires. In the end, it was not the lustful desire for sex I needed victory from, but my perversion of what God made holy. I had to reprogram my mind because selfishness was the real issue, not sex. I was cynical because my prayers were misguided. Once I realized the error of my ways, victory became a reality. I learned to relinquish control to God and my life drastically changed because I prayed by faith, not sight.

Application

1. When are you most tempted to look at life from a cynical, glass-half-empty perspective?

2. In what ways has your poor attitude impacted those around you? How often are you negative?

3. Why is it easier to vent your frustrations to loved ones rather than confess your thoughts to God in prayer?

4. Give an example (past or present) where cynicism created a wall between you and God. What did you learn as a result?

5. If cynicism is merely a smokescreen to justify not praying, what are you attempting to hide or run away from?

6. Do you believe prayer has no impact on the trials plaguing your life right now? Why or why not?

7. Which conditions or expectations that you place upon God fuel cynicism and draw you away from praying daily?

Prayer

Lord, I never realized how cynical I can be when I choose to go my own way rather than pray. My poor attitude has plagued our relationship together. I confess that I have leaned far more on my own understanding than submitting my will to Yours. Help me to stop looking at life from a glass-half-empty perspective and give thanks for the blessings You continually pour out on me. When I am tired and weary, draw me into Your presence where hope and healing are found. You are able to do abundantly more than I could ever ask for or imagine, so convict me of my unbelief. Amen.

Day 22 – Patience

Remedy: I wait for the Lord, my soul waits.

"I wait for the LORD, my soul waits, and in his word I hope;
my soul waits for the Lord more than watchmen for the morning,
more than watchmen for the morning."

— *Psalm 130:5–6* —

I hate waiting. I get easily agitated and restless when things take much longer than expected. My mood tends to worsen and my words develop a sharp edge when I feel inconvenienced. It is not hard for my family to see my patience wearing thin because I often wear my emotions on my sleeve. For better or worse, I fail to hide my true feelings but express them openly with no filter to buffer the blunt impact of my opinions. I am not proud of my anxious behavior. I wish I was more patient because I know that my attitude is contagious. God instructs me to lead by example, yet what I often model is not patience but a complete lack of self-control when things do not turn out how I think they should.

Patience is a fruit of the Spirit (Gal. 5:22-23). It is a gift from God to those who surrender to His authority, obey His Word, and submit to His sovereign will. It is the evidence of our faith commitment to Christ, to which others should be able to look at our behavior and know we live to honor the Lord in everything we say and do. For example, how we manage our time is an easy way to determine how flexible we are (or not) when life takes unexpected turns. Do we react with frustration or respond with understanding? The same concept applies to prayer when God does not answer in the manner which we prefer or expect.

Case in point, I once called on a retail chain that was financially unstable to say the least. After being forced to relocate my family once before due to the consolidation of two business units, I found myself staring at the possibility that my account would collapse and force my family into another relocation. As a result, I shifted gears and targeted a higher-profile account I could manage in an area that would allow me to work from home and be within driving distance of extended family. Ironically, there was only one dot on the map which made sense for us, so I made it known to my management team that I was ready and willing to relocate if the position became available.

Needless to say, the possibility kicked my prayer life into gear. I understood there were no guarantees, but it did not mean God was unable to make it happen. The challenge was that my desire was completely open-ended. It could have come to fruition, but it could not be forced either. I had to wait because it was in the Lord's hands and His timing is always perfect. Moreover, I could not fall into the trap of assuming the sales position was mine even if it did become available. It would have been arrogant for me to believe I was the only qualified applicant who deserved the job. In the end, the Lord did make a way, but I learned a hard lesson on the importance of patience to endure seasons of waiting.

We must remember that patience develops over time. We would not plant a seed in the ground and expect to yield a harvest the next day. That would be foolish. Proper growth takes time and requires sunlight, water, and fertilizer to ensure the seed develops correctly. However, when it comes to spiritual disciplines such as patience, we expect God to provide it without having to wait. Why? Would we understand the true value of patience if we never experienced the unpredictability of expectations?

In many ways, the struggle of waiting magnifies why patience is so priceless. It gives meaning and purpose to seasons of delay and makes us appreciate the mountaintop view when we work hard to reach our summit. It also illustrates the value of avoiding negativity, expectations, bitterness, and complaining, which are all reflective of prayer and applying the absolute truth of God's Word daily. In other words, we cannot achieve wisdom if we do not ask God (Jam. 1:5), and we will never understand the power of patience if we never experience seasons of trial and discomfort which force us to use wisdom and self-control.

In the grand scheme of things, I have learned that God answers prayer whenever and however He pleases. He is sovereign overall, so being impatient and demanding answers solves nothing. It only emboldens a negative attitude. As a result, I have shifted the angle of my conversations with God from "Please, grant me _____," to "Lord, if the answer is 'No,' help me understand why." This shift in strategy has been invaluable to helping me guard against placing ultimatums and expectations on God. The last thing I want to do is paint Him into a corner, but I can easily fall for that trap when I grow weary of waiting on answers. In turn, my prayers must be open to whatever the Lord desires and wherever He leads.

Inevitably, we do not need to be reminded of why patience is so important. The consequences of impatience communicate why it is an invaluable fruit of the Spirit. Far too many of us have wounds which stretch far and wide, made possible by our inability to wait for the Lord as He sees fit. That does not mean watching the clock is easy. It can be torturous to sit comfortably still and trust that His timing is always perfect. Even so, if we remind ourselves that all things work together for those who love God, perhaps trusting His sovereignty would not prove so difficult but manageable.

Application

1. Would you consider yourself a patient person? Why or why not?

2. How can you guard against negativity, bitterness, and complaining when your prayers are not answered the way you prefer?

3. Do you view patience as a gift from God or a skill you develop over time? How so?

4. Why do expectations fuel impatience?

5. What are the dangers of placing expectations on God when you offer prayer requests to Him?

6. How can praying for understanding rather than outcomes help you guard against placing ultimatums on God?

7. Which consequences of actions still haunt you to this day based on your impatience?

8. How has God taught you to value patience differently?

Prayer

Lord, as much as I look at patience from a me-centered lens, thank You for being so understanding. The grace You continually pour out upon me is nothing short of miraculous. I do not deserve Your gift of love and forgiveness. Please help me extend the same level of patience to others which You show me each day. I cannot possess the fruit of Your Spirit without investing quality time and energy praying without expectations and washing my mind with the water of Your Word. There is much wisdom in trusting the process, and I commit my heart, mind, and soul to You. Help me rest in the seasons of waiting that You sovereignly ordain for my life. Amen.

Day 23 – Hopelessness
Excuse: God doesn't care about me.

"May the God of hope fill you with all joy and peace in believing,
so that by the power of the Holy Spirit you may abound in hope."

— Romans 15:13 —

When we've reached the point where we doubt whether God cares about us, it is safe to say we have drifted off course and are on the verge of disaster. Like a ship without a rudder, we are subject to wherever the wind blows our faith. Our sense of direction is severely impaired and we have no idea where our true north lies. It can be a frightening experience to fall into despair and abandon hope in Christ completely. Satan thrives in such an isolated environment because we are entirely vulnerable. Truly, any vessel which has lost its ability to navigate properly is subject to shipwreck, and we are no different in our journey of faith if we give up praying to the Lord as well.

Hope is a powerful tool in the life of a Christ-follower. It can set the trajectory of our attitude and keep our attention laser-focused on Jesus despite our trials. Hopefulness looks at our problems from a glass-half-full perspective and searches for the silver lining of God's grace. It does not ignore difficulties but embraces them, for pain helps us appreciate the Lord's sovereignty and the lessons He wishes to teach us. Hope makes divine intervention precious in our sight because we recognize how much we do not deserve the Lord's favor. In turn, our belief that all things work together for those who trust in God and call upon His name for salvation comes to fruition, because we know He always has our best interest in mind.

Hopelessness is the exact opposite. It lacks faith and trust in the sovereignty of God which gives purpose and meaning to our trials. It thrives upon complaining and negativity, giving opportunity to bitterness and driving doubt deeper into our hearts and minds. When we yield to hopelessness, we cannot see the forest through the trees. Our perspective is so shortsighted that we fail to recognize what God has in store to teach us through pain and difficulty. Living from a glass-half-empty perspective is indeed depressing because we are always waiting for the other shoe to drop and expecting bad things to happen.

When I look back upon my addiction to pornography, nothing felt satisfying. No matter how many times I yielded to fleshly desire, nothing quenched my thirst for contentment. The world's pleasures did not satisfy and my heart plunged into a state of hopelessness for many years. Granted, I prayed to the Lord that He would release me from the chains of sin's bondage, but as soon as He would guard me from traveling down an even darker path, I would relapse and revert back to where I started. I could not build positive momentum and avoid yielding to temptation, so I gave up hope that tomorrow could be any different.

The problem was that I wanted an easy fix, so I prayed that way. I did not want to work for positive change. Rather, I expected God to push a reset button and reprogram my brain like it never happened. Unfortunately, the escape I hoped for never transpired. I assumed He did not care because my prayers were not answered as I expected. I was like a man recovering from injury who did not want to think or act differently. I just wanted Him to remove my sinful desires so I did not have to. However, because He didn't, I had all the more reason to believe that He could care less about my struggles. In my mind, I was all alone, so I gave up entirely on God.

Hopelessness is dangerous because it is grounded in unbelief. In our darkest moments, we desire momentary reprieve from the pain we experience, but our focus tends to be completely awry. It is as if we are languishing in hell and are more concerned about getting a drink of water than receiving salvation. Sadly, many of us cannot fathom that change is possible when despair consumes our minds. We become so content with desperation that we allow Satan full access to our hearts. Before we know it, he can twist our affections against the Lord and cause us to distrust the love of Christ.

It is easy to doubt whether God genuinely cares about us when we pray without ceasing and nothing seems to happen. Impatience is often a precursor to hopelessness and despair. Agitation leads to frustration causing seeds of impatience to grow until they have fully developed into full-blown rebellion. That is often why we believe Satan's lie that God could care less about us. Nevertheless, nothing in Scripture leads us to believe that Christ is absent in our darkest hour. Actually, **"The LORD is near to the brokenhearted and saves the crushed in spirit" (Psalm 34:18)**. In our moment of need, the Lord is ever-present and cares more about our well-being than we could ever imagine.

I deeply regret times when I have prayed and received silence in return. Reason being, I believed the lie that God was indifferent to my heart's cry because my circumstances did not change. I placed expectations on how, when, and where the Lord should act. If He didn't, I walked away and gave up praying. Truly, there is nothing more childish than pouting like a baby and hopelessly complaining when I fail to get my way. Thus, being hopeful is contingent upon trusting the Lord to do as He pleases, not as I will. For my trials and circumstances may not change, but I can rest easy knowing He is always in complete control, not me.

Application

1. How have you bought into Satan's lie that God does not care about you or your problems?

2. Do you pray more when you feel hopeless? Why or why not?

3. Are you typically more hopeful or hopeless when facing trials of many kinds? How so?

4. Why is despair so cancerous to a healthy prayer life?

5. How has hopelessness hindered your prayers?

6. How have unmet expectations soured your attitude toward God and hindered you from trying to pray?

7. Why is Psalm 34:18 a powerful verse to remember when you are wallowing in despair?

8. How can you guard against giving up on prayer when the Lord remains silent?

Prayer

Lord, hopelessness is a struggle for me. On one hand, I know You are sovereign and that all things work together for my good, but I cannot see the forest through the trees right now. The trials I am facing are so complicated and intense that I am hard-pressed to find a silver-lining. Your Word tells me to trust when I cannot see the other side of the horizon, but I am scared of what the future holds. What if things do not change for the better? What if they turn for the worst? How can I remain hopeful when despair is crouching at my door, seeking to take my heart captive? Thus, help me preach the Gospel to myself, so I do not fall prey to hopelessness. Amen.

Day 24 – Comfort
Remedy: Your rod and Your staff comfort me.

"Even though I walk through the valley of the shadow of death,
I will fear no evil, for you are with me;
your rod and your staff, they comfort me."

— Psalm 23:4 —

When we are overwhelmed by stress and anxiety, it is easy to succumb to doubt and lose hope that tomorrow will be any different. If we have been praying for the Lord to intervene in our trials and nothing seems to happen, we can easily feel defeated. We may assume our prayers do not align with God's will or that maybe they do, but His timing is different than ours. Trusting that God will answer our cries for help means we must relinquish control of how, when, or if He will act. All we can do is release our grip and allow Jesus to take the wheel, but that is easier said than done. What we need is comfort to survive another day and understanding to accept whatever the Lord has in store for the future.

Trials are inevitable. We cannot avoid them no matter how hard we try. What we can avoid, though, is defaulting into hopelessness when we feel as if the walls are closing in. Trials have meaning and purpose. God uses them to mold and define our character. Only the Lord knows the true intent of our hardships which reinforces why we must trust Him and not rely upon our own understanding. The challenge is we want to know why we are struggling and when our pain will subside. We long to know there is light at the end of the tunnel or a pot of gold at the end of the rainbow to give meaning and clarity to the sacrifices we must make along the way.

The problem is that answers take time and we do not like to wait too long if we can help it. We prefer a solution now (good or bad) so we can wrap our minds around what we are facing and begin to strategize next steps. Health concerns are a primary example of what we all face on occasion. When we feel sick, we seek medical advice to help identify and resolve the problem. Our end goal is to work towards a solution, so expecting excruciating pain to go away with little to no intervention is not a viable option. Rather, we want to wrap our minds around the big picture of what we are facing to help narrow our focus and figure out how we will respond.

What happens, though, when we have exhausted all options and are stuck in neutral? What if we have remained patient and hopeful despite our difficulties but no change has occurred? In many ways, it comes down to washing our minds with the truth of God's Word which reminds us that He is in complete control. Psalm 23 is an example of how King David quieted his mind and comforted his heart by reminding himself of God's character. **"The LORD is my shepherd; I shall not want. He makes me lie down in green pastures. He leads me beside still waters. He restores my soul. He leads me in paths of righteousness for his name's sake"** **(Psalm 23:1–3)**.

David did not require God to answer his prayers in any certain way. What he desired was comfort despite his trials—to know that the Lord would never leave or forsake him but guide his path unto righteousness. He knew that if God stood beside him, no one could ultimately harm him, so he trusted the Lord rather than his feelings to guide his actions. David understood that the eye of the storm was the greatest place to experience calm and achieve peace, so he rested in the shadow of the Most High and washed his mind with the water of holy Scripture to affirm and strengthen his faith.

The apostle Paul put it this way, **"Who shall separate us from the love of Christ? Shall tribulation, or distress, or persecution, or famine, or nakedness, or danger, or sword?" (Romans 8:35). "No, in all these things we are more than conquerors through him who loved us" (Romans 8:37)**. It is easy to lose hope in God when we believe our problems are bigger than what He can handle. However, the Bible reminds us that we are more than conquerors over the forces of darkness when we stop fighting our battles and allow the Lord to intervene. When we do, we can rest easy because our comfort is in Christ alone. Satan holds no power over us if we are washed in the blood of the Lamb. Hence, we must relinquish control of our lives to Jesus at all times.

When my wife had a miscarriage between our third and fourth daughters, we were devastated by the loss but understood that God was still in control. What we did not expect were the complications which ensued, requiring Amber to be rushed to the hospital after calling 911. She had lost too much blood at home and passed out as a result. It was a terrifying experience seeing my wife lie in a pool of blood on the bathroom floor only to have a group of firemen rush into our home and immediately whisk her away to save her life.

I can remember feeling helpless in that moment. I had to quickly arrange for my older daughters to stay with friends so I could get to the hospital. I had no clue what was going on until I arrived. All I could do was trust Jesus because my wife was far more precious to Him than to me and was safe in His sovereign care. In that moment, the Lord heard my cries for Amber's healing and gave me comfort. She suffered traumatically, but it did not crush her spirit. Rather, her faith in Christ was emboldened because she knew the Lord would guide her path. In the end, she trusted Him completely and comfort overwhelmed her heart and mind in that moment as well.

Application

1. How have you experienced God's comfort in the midst of trials and hardship (even when it was not blatantly obvious)?

2. Why would the rod and staff of God be comforting if you walk through the valley of the shadow of death?

3. What does the comfort of God look like in prayer?

4. Give an example of a time when you trusted the Lord but your situation did not change. How did you not yield to hopelessness but instead trust His sovereignty despite the trial you faced?

5. Do you believe that nothing can separate you from the love of Christ? How have your life experiences affirmed your position?

6. Why is the comfort of Jesus Christ critical to surviving spiritual warfare and enduring seasons of trial?

7. How has the Lord comforted you in your hour of despair? What has He taught you about trusting the power of His Word?

Prayer

Lord, Your Word is a lamp to my feet and a light to my path. Thank You for continuing to love me during my darkest hours and comforting me when I could not see the light at the end of my trials. You have been so gracious when I have allowed my emotions to get the best of me. Please help me to continue running to You in prayer and laying my cares and concerns at Your feet. I do not want to feel enslaved to hopelessness any longer. Instead, help me trust Your will when I cannot predict the future. You always know what is best, Lord, so I will relinquish control and find comfort in You. Amen.

Day 25 – Distance
Excuse: I can't hear God when I pray.

"Whoever is of God hears the words of God. The reason why you do not hear them is that you are not of God."

— *John 8:47* —

There comes a point in each of our lives when we cannot seem to hear the Lord speaking. It is a gradual degradation process whereby His voice becomes faint as time goes on. The challenge is our world is so full of noise and static that unless we lock ourselves in a soundproof room, we will never know what it feels like to sit in solitude. As we studied on Day-15, distractions sway our attention from quality time in prayer to a smorgasbord of priorities which compete with the Lord. Every time we say, "Yes!" to a distraction, God is left in the waiting room of our hearts indefinitely. How then can we keep our frequencies clear so that when God does speak, we recognize His voice and obey His Word?

Time is the great equalizer of life. For example, it has been over twenty years since my mother passed away from cancer. She died at the age of sixty-three, far too young for a woman who lived the right way and never abused her body. Outside of my wife, my mother is the greatest woman I have ever known. I loved her dearly, and it still hurts to this day that she is gone. I have often wondered, and even dreamt on occasion, what it would be like to spend one more day with her. I miss her smile and warm hugs, her incredible cooking and heart for others. She was a Proverbs 31 woman of God in many ways, and I was incredibly blessed to spend the first twenty-five years of my life with her.

Regrettably, though she will always be close to my heart, I have lost the ability to hear her voice. It has become a faint recollection in my mind. All I have are distant memories because she has been gone for so long, and I will not see her again until we are reunited in heaven one day. Similarly, the ability to hear applies to my prayer life as well. Time has created a barrier of distance between myself and God. I struggle discerning whether He is even speaking to me at times. How can that be? If I call myself a Christian, how can the Lord's voice be as unfamiliar to me as that of a complete stranger?

In many ways, we tend to think of our relationship with God like a game of pitch and catch. We can be standing in the middle of a football field, tossing the ball back and forth to one another, and having a conversation while doing it. Dialogue is effortless so long as we maintain a close distance to enjoy our time together and hear what the other is saying. What happens, though, when that 10-yard distance between us expands? We can still have a conversation from twenty or even thirty yards away, but what if we extend to the full length of the field? Can we still hear God clearly when distance is too much to bear?

The sad truth is many of us are not standing on opposite ends of the field in prayer. We are actually standing on opposite ends of the top row in a large capacity stadium. There is no way we can hear the Lord from that distance because we have not invested quality time building a relationship with Him which can stand the test of time. Instead, we believe we can casually check in with Him a few times a month and maintain an intimate relationship. Would that strategy work in marriage, though, if a husband and wife barely spoke to one another? Of course not, but we act as if we can do the bare minimum communicating yet complain when we cannot hear the Lord's voice amongst all the static in our lives.

Undoubtedly, we have a multitude of people, places, and things vying for our attention. We may be married with kids, have elderly parents living with us, work a full-time job, or maintain a variety of activities to keep ourselves engaged in the community. All are justifiable priorities, yet none would be possible outside of the Lord's provision. Without Him, we are empty and possess nothing of true value. Our ability to live and breathe is contingent upon His grace, so why would we allow distance to come between us? The farther away we are from His presence, the greater likelihood we will not receive the wisdom He wishes to share with us.

Prayer is our ultimate measuring device to track how far away we are from the Lord. If we cannot find time to pray, our ability to hear Him calling will become extremely difficult. We will struggle recognizing the sound of His voice and potentially mistake Satan for an angel of light (2 Cor. 11:14) who speaks on the Lord's behalf. There are many dangers with being so far disconnected from God in prayer that we open ourselves up to spiritual warfare. The enemy thrives upon such confusion, for not being able to accurately discern the Lord's voice can leave us vulnerable to attack.

In the end, distance is one of the easiest problems in prayer to remedy as increased frequency can help close the gap to hear God more clearly. However, both quantity and quality of time are critical to success. We must not only carve out time for Him but make the most of the time we invest. Jesus made it clear that those who are of God know Him and hear His voice distinctly. As a result, there should be no confusion about whether He is speaking if we have developed a close, personal relationship with Him over time. In turn, we are wise to ensure that distance does not pull us so far away from God that we give up on prayer and assume He is either not listening or does not care about us altogether.

Application

1. Which is more important: quality time or quantity of time? Why?

2. How would you describe your personal relationship with God? How close or distant do you feel from Him on a daily basis?

3. Which trials have tempted you to maintain your distance from God rather than draw near to Him for refuge?

4. What role has time played in your ability to accurately discern the Lord's voice?

5. How often do you talk to God in prayer for a substantial length of time? Why?

6. What do you communicate when you prioritize people, places, or things above quality time with the Lord?

7. Is God's voice distinct in your life or do you struggle recognizing it from a distance? How so?

Prayer

Lord, at times I find myself far away from Your presence. When I stop and reflect upon the time I invest in our relationship, it is easy to see why I feel so disconnected. I have allowed everything under the sun to monopolize my attention, and the residual impact is that my prayer life is hit or miss. I am a victim of busyness with no one to blame but myself. I chose to allow idols to come between us and I repent of my foolishness. Help me discover the joy of my salvation in You. My life would be void of true happiness if You were not in it. Also, please instill a newfound hunger for prayer in my heart and help me guard against allowing distance to draw us apart. Amen.

Day 26 – Intimacy
Remedy: Pray to your Father who is in secret.

"But when you pray, go into your room,
shut the door, and pray to your Father who is in secret.
And your Father who sees in secret will reward you."

— *Matthew 6:6* —

It is easy to feel that God is a mile away when we fail to prioritize prayer. Creating an environment for spiritual intimacy to flourish is no small feat. It can be difficult finding the right time and place to talk to God without distractions. Distance can be cancerous to a healthy prayer life, which means prayer is hypercritical to fixing the problem. The challenge is whether or not we want to develop a personal relationship with God in the first place. Intimacy with the Father should be a foregone conclusion in the life of a Christian, but some of us would rather keep God at arm's length until we need Him. Sadly, we are disinterested in sacrificing our time and energy to grow spiritually, but this is often why we feel discontent as well.

It may be a tough pill to swallow, but we must ask ourselves whether we even want to know God more. In other words, do we understand the residual benefits of an ongoing personal relationship with Jesus Christ? Will we carve out more time for prayer and make sacrifices to our schedules, if needed, to develop intimacy with Him? Are we committed to developing spiritual disciplines, no matter the cost? For some people, simply wanting to pray more is where the rubber meets the road. For others, consistency is key. No matter the issues we may be facing, God is always eager to spend time with us. As such, the ball is in our court to pursue a relationship with Him.

Learning to pray has been a bottleneck in my faith journey. My Dad never taught me how, so I did not understand what a personal relationship with Christ meant. All I knew was religion and rules to follow. That is not to say I blame my Dad for my faith struggles, but I see how the bond I had with my earthly father impacted my relationship with God. My Dad was very private in his Catholic faith. I never saw him pray at home because he would always lean on my Mom to carry the load of spiritual formation and handle faith discussions. Getting him to open up about his theology made him extremely uncomfortable. I never understood why, so I avoided talking about the Bible with him because he felt intimidated by it.

It is interesting to see the correlation between my struggles with prayer and the difficulty of engaging my Dad in faith conversations. My poor attitude with prayer is reminiscent of how I interacted with him. I did not know how to remedy it, so I gave up hope that we could ever be close. He recently passed away, almost twenty years after my Mom lost her battle to cancer, but I regret that we never had the relationship we could have had if he had been willing to open himself up and lead me spiritually. In retrospect, I see how I acted similarly toward God. Because of my discomforts with prayer, I shut the Lord out like my Dad did to me. Pride got the best of me, but I no longer want to live that way moving forward.

It can be difficult to admit that what we need more than anything is to lock ourselves in a closet, turn off the lights, and focus all our attention on the Lord. There should be no ulterior motive fueling our behavior except a genuine desire to share our hearts with God and receive His wisdom and counsel in return. That is why Jesus taught His disciples to pray in secret, not that public prayer is wrong but rather that time developing deep intimacy with God should be reserved for private settings. Granted, if we have children, they need to see us model a discipline of prayer. Still, our motivation cannot be to portray ourselves as more righteous than we truly are but to humble ourselves before the Lord and set a good example.

It can feel awkward developing spiritual intimacy with God. As men, culture has taught us to hide our feelings, stuff our emotions, and avoid vulnerability under any circumstance. Learning to express ourselves is often shunned and persecuted, so there is a mental hurdle we must overcome to change our misperception about intimacy. Keep in mind, growing our relationship with God through prayer means we are willing to call a spade a spade and admit our failures. There is no need to sugarcoat the reality of how wretched and depraved we are. Rather, we can humble ourselves before God and repent of our sins, giving Him ample opportunity to forgive and discipline us as He sees fit.

Intimacy entails sharing our fears, doubts, and worries before the Lord as well. We can bear our souls before Him because we know healing is found when we lay our burdens down at the foot of the cross. That is the Good News of the Gospel. We are saved by grace by the blood of the Lamb and will stand blameless before our Father in heaven one day. Therefore, intimacy is a golden opportunity to trade our sorrow for joy. Scripture affirms, **"There is now no condemnation for those who are in Christ Jesus" (Romans 8:1)**, and we are wise to receive His gift of salvation for eternity.

In the end, the more we lean upon prayer and open our hearts to the Lord, the more we will experience intimacy with our heavenly Father. Intimacy is developed over time when we invest generously to receive a profitable return. That logic applies financially and it correlates spiritually as well when we tithe the first fruits of our time and energy to the Lord in prayer. All we must do to close the distance gap is simply be present in the moment.

Application

1. Do you want to know God more? Why or why not?

2. How has intimacy with God been modeled to you growing up? If you lacked a godly example, what impact has that had?

3. What correlation exists between your earthly father's example and how you see and interact with your heavenly Father?

4. Why is it necessary to have uninterrupted, 1-on-1 time with the Lord in prayer?

5. Do you have a quiet location or prayer closet reserved for quality time with God? Why or why not?

6. How has a lack of consistency with time hindered your ability to pray more intimately?

7. What hurdles must you overcome to change your misperception about spiritual intimacy?

Prayer

Lord, it seems as if it should be so easy to talk to You, but I often struggle finding the words to express how I am thinking and feeling. You already know what is on my heart and mind, but I often get uncomfortable and intimidated talking to You and inevitably walk away. Rather than run to my prayer closet, I avoid it or allow busyness to monopolize my time. Please help me to get out of my head and embrace the opportunity to grow closer to You. Help me seek after intimacy with You and not shy away from it. I long to know You more but struggle discerning what that looks like, so help me trust Your Spirit and engage prayer more frequently. Amen.

Day 27 – Repetition

Excuse: I just repeat myself when I pray.

"And when you pray, do not heap up empty phrases as the Gentiles do, for they think that they will be heard for their many words."

— *Matthew 6:7* —

Have you ever felt like a broken record when you pray? I have. For whatever reason, I default into autopilot mode when I pray and rattle off the same prayer requests repeatedly. I do the same thing with praises, yet the repetitive nature of prayer bothers me so much that it makes me not want to pray. In my mind, I am tired of hearing the same concerns come out of my mouth. Surely God feels the same, right? That is at least what I rationalize in my head to justify my negative attitude. Being repetitive troubles me because it seems like I have nothing else to say other than, "Thank You for dying on a cross for my sins and blessing me beyond measure. Please keep my family safe and healthy. Amen."

What is wrong with repetitive prayers, though, if they are truly how we feel? Nothing. God never tires of hearing us thank Him for His sovereign provision, and He appreciates our care and concern for the needs of others as well. Why then do we walk away from prayer because it feels repetitive? The answer begins and ends with spiritual warfare. Satan is focused on drawing us away from God's presence with false assumptions and confusion. Therefore, it should not surprise us when he manipulates our minds to avoid spiritual disciplines to stunt our growth. Under the guise of expectations, He wants us to reflect upon how we fall short of righteousness so we give up hope on the possibility of a vibrant prayer life.

Repetition in prayer is not a bad thing unless we are attempting to pacify the Lord by checking off a legalistic box. God knows the true intent of our hearts, so using repetition as an excuse to avoid being vulnerable is lazy and foolish. Case in point, we rarely think the same exact thoughts each day because tomorrow is different. Perspectives change, personal experience increases, and our character evolves over time. We always have something new to pray about, so why do we default to the same laundry list of prayers? It would be equivalent to asking our children, "How was your day?" and their response is always, "Fine."

Our time on earth is full of exciting adventures and painstaking trials. Not a day goes by that our emotions do not ebb and flow to some degree. We have so much to talk about with God, yet we default to the same canned speech and deny Him the opportunity to hear us tell Him what is on our hearts and minds. Why? It would be like owning an ice cream shop, having numerous exotic flavors to choose from, but only giving God a small sample of plain old vanilla to appease Him. Granted, there is nothing wrong with vanilla. God is simply longing to enjoy every flavor we have at our disposal. Thus, we must be willing to share all we have with Him.

The Lord never grows tired or weary of hearing us pray a familiar cadence if we enjoy and feel comfortable reciting it that way. There is safety and security having structure and a framework for prayer. However, we cannot offer God a minimum effort and expect spiritual revival to ignite in our hearts. We must engage the process to receive a good return on our investment. It would be similar to having a detailed Bible study journal in hand with great questions to chew on but only writing down one-word answers. Why? God has given us ample opportunity to share our thoughts with Him, yet we tend to keep our cards close rather than expound upon them.

Sometimes, we are our own worst enemy. We get in our heads far too much and give up developing an intimate relationship with God because we assume prayer has to look a certain way to be effective. Repetitive prayer can be helpful to some degree but challenging ourselves to expand our spiritual discipline boundaries and open our hearts is healthy. It allows God to prune the dead branches from our lives so we can develop new growth and a bountiful harvest. **"I am the true vine, and my Father is the vinedresser. Every branch in me that does not bear fruit he takes away, and every branch that does bear fruit he prunes, that it may bear more fruit" (John 15:1–2).**

Currently, I am in the middle of a pruning season. For too long, I bought the lie that repetitiveness in prayer was a big problem. I believed that I had to stop repeating myself because monotony was foolish and ineffective. I allowed Satan to bait me into believing that repetitive prayer had no value which inevitably deterred me from overcoming my insecurities years ago. I have long been enslaved to unrealistic expectations which are nothing more than a figment of my imagination. God has never chastised me for how I pray to Him, yet I felt like I needed to be more eloquent in how I prayed. That only drew me further away instead of closer to Him, and I deeply regret buying into the enemy's schemes so easily.

Our heavenly Father longs for us to come to Him with humble hearts and a genuine willingness to bear our souls daily. In turn, we are wise to abandon our misconceptions about what He expects and freely open our hearts to Him without reservation. For the day will come when we will stand before God, and the last thing we want to hear is **"I never knew you; depart from me" (Matthew 7:23).** Therefore, let us avoid heaping big words and empty phrases upon God and instead, offer our hearts to Him in reverence to Christ.

Application

1. Is your prayer life monotonous or repetitive? Which praises or prayer requests do you consistently offer up to God?

2. Have you believed Satan's lie that repetitive prayer is ineffective? Why or why not?

3. What do you believe God thinks about your repetitive prayers? How has that impacted your approach (for better or worse)?

4. How can you guard against legalistically pacifying God with your prayers rather than looking forward to praying with Him?

5. Considering the ice cream example, how often do you give God "vanilla" prayers instead of multiple flavors?

6. Do you believe prayer must look like or sound a certain way to be effective? How so?

7. How often do you heap up empty phrases to God rather than humble, genuine repentance? Why?

Prayer

Lord, there are pros and cons to repetitive prayer. I am certainly on a journey of sorts discovering where I should invest my efforts to pray more effectively with You. I realize that You are far less concerned with my words than the condition of my heart. Help me overcome my fear of being vulnerable with You. It is easy to default into repetitive mode, so teach me to step out in faith and expand my comfort level. I do not want to settle for vanilla prayers. Rather, help me offer my thoughts and intentions to You, unconditionally and without hesitation. Amen.

Day 28 – Balance

Remedy: For everything, there is a season.

"For everything there is a season, and a time for every matter under heaven: a time to be born, and a time to die; a time to plant, and a time to pluck up what is planted; a time to kill, and a time to heal; a time to break down, and a time to build up; a time to weep, and a time to laugh; a time to mourn, and a time to dance; a time to cast away stones, and a time to gather stones together; a time to embrace, and a time to refrain from embracing; a time to seek, and a time to lose; a time to keep, and a time to cast away; a time to tear, and a time to sew; a time to keep silence, and a time to speak; a time to love, and a time to hate; a time for war, and a time for peace."

— Ecclesiastes 3:1–8 —

If repetition hinders us from achieving lasting contentment with prayer, then balance is the remedy to save us from monotony. As King Solomon eloquently wrote, there is a time and season for everything. Nothing in our lives falls outside the boundary of God's sovereignty. Every trial we face has a distinct purpose to sanctify our hearts and purify our souls. Our sufferings connect us to Jesus who died in our place and gave His life as a ransom for our freedom. As such, while our sins invoke the wrath of God's eternal judgment, Christ's blood washes us clean so we can stand blameless before the throne of grace.

Balance is a foundational aspect of God's righteous character. The picture of His love satisfying His need for justice is incredible. God's grace is amazing because His wrath against sin is so intense. One cannot exist without the other, and we are the beneficiaries of those balanced scales. How then do we avoid taking for granted the trials which God allows? If He has given us everything we need as it pertains to life and godliness, could the seasons of pain and hardship we face not be a part of His master plan too?

The simple truth is that balance is key to spiritual survival. Just as repetition is not inherently wrong, falling prey to monotony is not what God wants for us either. He longs for us to discover balance in our prayers and not just camp out in one area but expand our horizons. Jesus sought to instill structure into our quiet time with the Father, which many refer to as the ACTS model of prayer. Based on the structure of the Lord's Prayer, Adoration, Confession, Thanksgiving, and Supplication are the areas we should focus on to find balance. Not to say that leaning more into one area is bad but finding rhythm between all four helps ensure we focus our minds vertically and horizontally.

Adoration is all about praising God for who He is. It centers our minds on the majesty of His holiness and yields our hearts to the Spirit's providential control. When we adore God, we give Him the honor and glory He is due and submit ourselves to His sovereignty. Even so, just as we turn our heads to heaven in adoration, we must also bow our heads and reflect upon our heart's depravity. We simply cannot stand before the Lord's presence on judgment day without receiving atonement for our sins. Therefore, confession must be a critical aspect of our daily prayer to accompany adoration.

God does not expect us to beat ourselves up, though, by wallowing in guilt and shame. Rather, He encourages us to own our sins and mourn the damages we caused with selfless perspective. When we assume our sins exist in a vacuum, we separate ourselves from the cross of Calvary. Yet, when we embrace godly grief and accept the consequences of our actions, transformation occurs. As a result, we must always be thankful. For we were once dead in our sins, but

Christ set us free by the power of His shed blood to reconcile our hearts to the Father forevermore.

More specifically, we offer thanks to God in prayer because all we have and who we are is solely a result of His grace and mercy. We do not deserve the bountiful blessings He graciously provides, but we receive them in humility because our eternal debt was paid once and for all. That is the Good News of the Gospel which we rejoice in as born-again followers of Jesus Christ. If nothing more, thankfulness should pour out from us on a daily basis. For we have been given victory over sin and death through the cross of Calvary, and that is easily worth celebrating every day of our lives.

Once we have established adoration, confession, and thanksgiving in our prayers, we have ample opportunity to offer our petitions to the Lord. What a glorious privilege! The Creator of the universe loves us so much that He gives His full and undivided attention whenever we desire. It is amazing that He speaks to every soul who calls upon the name of Jesus for salvation. What more could we ask for? God has given us direct access to His heart. All we must do is freely express our thoughts to Him and not hold back what we are feeling at any given moment.

The more I have leaned into the ACTS model of prayer, stress and anxiety have decreased. When I quiet my mind and give God the time and attention He deserves by balancing my thoughts and expressing my feelings, I experience peace which transcends all understanding. I cannot explain how, but contentment washes over me when I intentionally praise God, confess my sins, thank Him for His blessings, and share my petitions. My perspective changes and prayer is no longer about me but Him. It is certainly not easy to shift gears, but I am improving my prayer life and leading my family better each day by giving God the glory He rightly deserves.

Application

1. Which season of life (feast or famine) do you find yourself in currently? How so?

2. How can you begin your prayers with adoration and glorify the Lord more often?

3. Which aspect of confession, if any, do you incorporate into your prayers? How can you mourn your sins before the Lord?

4. How can thankfulness be a defining attribute of your personal character as a Christ-follower?

5. Do you default to supplication (prayer requests) at the beginning or end of your prayers? Why?

6. How can you use the ACTS model of prayer more often? What needs to change?

7. Considering Ecclesiastes 3:1-8, why is balance in prayer critical to spiritual survival?

Prayer

Lord, I am sorely out of balance in my prayer life. I confess that I often jump to my laundry list of wants and desires before offering adoration, confession, and thanksgiving to You. I know that I need more balance in my life. I commit to ensuring I spend time daily glorifying You, confessing my sins, and giving You thanks before defaulting to prayer requests. I already have everything I need in this world because You saved my soul from damnation. Therefore, let me sing Your praises forevermore because You alone are worthy to be praised. Amen.

Day 29 – Boredom

Excuse: I don't enjoy praying. I feel nothing.

*"Slothfulness casts into a deep sleep,
and an idle person will suffer hunger."*

— Proverbs 19:15 —

It feels wrong to admit that we struggle finding a genuine desire to pray, but that is the unfortunate truth for many of us who call ourselves Christians. In a world of instant gratification where desires crave immediate satisfaction, waiting endlessly seems like cruel and unusual punishment. We struggle understanding how we can feel remotely satisfied talking to the Lord in what appears to be a one-sided conversation. From our perspective, we cannot easily relate to someone like Moses who spoke directly to God and received literal feedback in return. Rather, we are expected to listen for the Spirit's prompting in our hearts and discern the Bible's teachings to hear what the Lord has to say.

The reason many of us struggle with prayer is because we cannot tolerate silence. Our minds are accustomed to noise and sitting quietly does not interest us whatsoever. Spiritually-speaking, we tend to believe we have an attention-deficit disorder, making it easier to justify why we are bored with prayer. Conversely, being slothful is a whole different issue. We cannot expect to grow spiritually if we are unwilling to make a conscious effort. The challenge is we are often too busy and exhausted to focus our attention on God. As a result, we prove in moments of laziness that He is not important enough for us to change our ways and ignite spiritual revival in our hearts. If He was, we would not be so easily distracted.

I hate admitting it, but I struggle mightily with prayer boredom. My mind cannot get over the one-directional aspect of it. I long for the opportunity to have an audible discussion with the Lord, but that is not how prayer works. While it may seem like I am talking to a brick wall or releasing my thoughts into thin air, the reality is that God hears my cries. He knows the thoughts and intentions of my heart, so where is the disconnect? Why am I expecting Him to speak audibly in order for prayer to prove effective in my mind? The Lord can communicate to me however He chooses, so forcing unrealistic expectations upon Him will only promote bitterness and frustration in my heart.

I have often painted God into a box of my own creation to justify boredom. I did not want to admit that perhaps He could speak to me in extraordinary ways, but I had to be willing to relinquish my pride and do things His way. I held firm to the typical "it's my way or the highway" attitude, and that root of foolishness cost me years of intimate fellowship with the Lord. I was too stubborn to believe that God existed outside the framework of my expectations. I was also too busy justifying why I was so bored with prayer to ultimately solve the problem. It was not until I realized how laziness robbed the joy of my salvation that change took place.

Sometimes, we buy into a lie which says prayer must be as exciting as an action movie to be worth the price of admission. However, prayer is not entertainment but an opportunity to express our hearts and humble ourselves before the throne of grace. Prayer reminds us of the greatest love story ever told when God stepped down from heaven to save us from our sins. It affirms our devotion to Jesus Christ as the founder and perfecter of our faith. Prayer is actually the great antithesis of sloth and boredom because God revives us in our brokenness and breathes new life into our hearts.

To say we are bored with prayer is foolish. That only proves our spiritual immaturity and calls into question whether we understand what a faith relationship with Christ entails. Sadly, we often assume that God is disinterested with our lives. We rail against the silence we receive and assume He is too far away in our time of need. We believe He has little to no time for our insignificant lives, so we pack up, throw in the towel, and simply go home. I know I have made that decision repeatedly. Truly, many of us have checked out on prayer as well because we became bored waiting on God to answer in the time and manner we expected.

That truth can be an incredible epiphany in the life of a Christ-follower who struggles with prayer. Boredom is often a figment of our imagination in many ways. Like a genie in a bottle, we tend to rub our prayer lamps when we want something and expect God to grant our wishes. It is the ultimate example of pride, arrogance, and entitlement, yet we hold God accountable to unrealistic expectations all the time. We paint Him into a corner and then declare He is unloving when life does not turn out how we think it should. What does it say about us, though, when we reject His sovereignty because it feels boring?

The Lord is always in control no matter how we try to rationalize the complete opposite in our minds. He answers prayer as He sees fit based on His omniscient, sovereign perspective. As a result, if we have any chance of overcoming struggles with boredom in prayer, we must stop expecting God to conform to our way of thinking and instead, yield to His. It is certainly easier said than done, but the Lord is patient and longsuffering despite how often we give up on prayer. In the end, not every prayer moment we personally experience will move mountains, but it can be life-changing if we die to expectations and trust the Lord's sovereignty instead.

Application

1. Do you ever get bored with prayer? How so? What drives your discontentment?

2. How comfortable are you with waiting? What level of patience do you possess when you become bored praying to God?

3. How are laziness and boredom intertwined?

4. Do you view prayer as one-directional? Why or why not?

5. Why is it easy to fall into boredom with prayer when you place unrealistic expectations on how God should respond?

6. Why is it critical to guard against misinterpreting silence from the Lord through a negative light?

7. How often do you get tired of waiting on God to answer your prayers? What typically fuels your impatience?

Prayer

Lord, not a day goes by that I do not wonder whether my prayers will be answered. The plans You have for me are a mystery, so it can be difficult to trust what my future holds when I dwell upon present trials. Waiting is not a strength of mine either. I get easily frustrated when things do not work out quickly or how I think they should. Help me die to unrealistic expectations which paint You in a corner. I am so ashamed that I have treated You like a genie in a bottle, expecting You to grant my never-ending wish list without considering whether my will aligns with Yours. Please forgive my arrogance, Lord, and restore the joy of my salvation so that I never yield to boredom again. Amen.

Day 30 – Revival
Remedy: Taste and see that the Lord is good.

"Oh, taste and see that the LORD is good!
Blessed is the man who takes refuge in him!"

— *Psalm 34:8* —

Losing interest in prayer just happens sometimes. When we go through rainy seasons where our faith is drenched by countless trials, it can be difficult to remain joyful amid pain and suffering. We also experience dry seasons in our journey of faith which attack us from a different angle but are equally destructive. They are brought on by fatigue, laziness, and boredom, and help explain our disinterest with prayer and inability to find the silver-lining of God's grace through our trials. Both seasons require divine intervention to conquer the enemy and restore the joy of our salvation in Christ. Thus, if we are determined to overcome the obstacles set before us, we must open our hearts to spiritual revival and surrender control of our lives to the Lord alone.

Spiritual revival can be a difficult concept to wrap our minds around. As stated in my recent book, **"Lord, I'm Tired,"** spiritual revival originates from a genuine hunger and thirst for the Lord to stir our hearts, awaken our minds, and ignite the Spirit's fire within our souls. It is not something we manufacture by the sweat of our brow. Only God has the power to turn ashes to beauty and shed light into the darkness of our hearts. The problem is we often have no desire to relinquish control. We would rather exhaust every angle possible to save ourselves than throw our hands in the air and cry out, "Jesus, take the wheel!"

Admitting we have no power or authority to change our plight in life can be a hard pill to swallow. Pride wells up inside of us and we assume that life is what we make of it, not what God sovereignly ordains. Yet in the midst of our rebellion, we prove how much we need Him and why we struggle getting excited to pray. Oftentimes, we expect the earth to shake and the heavens to open up as a clear sign God is speaking, but that is not how He works. The Lord gently whispers inwardly through the Spirit by affirming what we read in Scripture. For if He has to grab our attention by means of action entertainment rather than Biblical revelation, it is safe to say we have completely missed the point.

Just as the Lord revealed Himself to the prophet, Elijah, we too must seek Him in the silence of prayer to clearly hear the Holy Spirit whispering to our souls. **"And he said, 'Go out and stand on the mount before the LORD.' And behold, the LORD passed by, and a great and strong wind tore the mountains and broke in pieces the rocks before the LORD, but the LORD was not in the wind. And after the wind an earthquake, but the LORD was not in the earthquake. And after the earthquake a fire, but the LORD was not in the fire. And after the fire the sound of a low whisper" (1 Kings 19:11–12).**

Spiritual revival begins and ends with an awakening in the depths of our souls where depravity is revealed. In that moment, we are laid bare before the judgment seat of Christ and recognize, perhaps for the first time, how desperately we need Him. That is where revival originates because we finally realize how incapable we are to save ourselves. Our minds are open to hearing the truth of Scripture and our hearts are willing to receive it. In other words, whether or not we feel comfortable praying, we are compelled to cry out to God and beg for His grace, mercy, and forgiveness.

I have long wrestled with what a "spiritual awakening" looks like. The challenge is that it is different for everyone. Just as every human being has a unique fingerprint, personal experiences are unique as well. The thread of God's grace is woven throughout the tapestry of my life in an exclusive pattern. What impacts me looks and feels different vs. everyone else. What I must remember, though, is that God speaks directly and indirectly through the divine revelation of His Word. For if what I read and hear does not align with Biblical truth, then God is not speaking. Therefore, I cannot assume I am having a revival experience if I fail to justify what I'm thinking and feeling with what the Bible teaches.

Many of us get bored having to filter what we believe through the pages of God's Word. We would rather make our own decisions and pick and choose what feels right to appease our flesh. Unfortunately, when we disregard absolute truth in favor of relativism, we easily fall into a state of confusion and struggle understanding why we need to pray or read the Bible at all. Satan knows that if God's Word takes root in our hearts, spiritual revival will begin to flourish. His main objective is to destroy absolute truth. Thus, if he can tempt us to doubt the validity of Scripture, we will only have a foundation of sinking sand to build our lives upon.

Truly, we must guard the moments we have with God in prayer each day. Time we invest into our personal relationship with Christ is priceless. When we open His Word and reflect upon who He is, why He came, and what He has done for us, we have all the fuel we need to ignite a fire of praise and adoration in our souls. Jesus saved us from eternal destruction! What more evidence do we need to turn our lives around and begin glorifying Him? We have been redeemed by the blood of the Lamb, and that ember has the power to not only ignite our hearts but the souls of others as well.

Application

1. What do you believe spiritual revival should look like in the heart of a born-again, Christ-follower?

2. Which season (dry or rainy) do you find yourself in today? How has that impacted your prayer life?

3. Do you believe life is more about what you make of it or what God sovereignly ordains? How so?

4. How does the Lord typically get your attention? What does He do (compared to what you expect Him to do)?

5. When was the last time you were laid bare before the judgment seat of Christ? How did you respond?

6. Why is Scriptural truth paramount to discerning whether God is speaking to you?

7. Why is spiritual revival dependent upon knowing who Jesus is, why He came, and what He has done for you?

Prayer

Lord, Your grace is amazing! I am humbled by Your love which rescues me from the depths of depravity. When I am lost, You give me purpose and direction, leading me home to Your presence. Help me not to sit and wait for mountains to move to know You are speaking. Instead, teach me to rest in the shelter of Your wings—to taste and see that You are always good. Spiritual revival is found when I am not swayed by seasons of trial or boredom but when I pray reverently, read Your Word, and submit to Your will. As such, ignite an ember of revival in me from this day forward. Amen.

Day 31 – Restriction

Excuse: I don't want to obey God's command.

"The LORD God took the man and put him in the garden of Eden to work it and keep it. And the LORD God commanded the man, saying, 'You may surely eat of every tree of the garden, but of the tree of the knowledge of good and evil you shall not eat, for in the day that you eat of it you shall surely die.'"

— Genesis 2:15–17 —

There is a motto I picked up from a friend of mine many years ago that I have used with my children to teach the importance of obedience. He would call out, "Listen and obey," and whichever child he was speaking to would always respond, "Right away!" I will never forget the first time I experienced that exchange. At first, it made me uncomfortable because it felt cold, strict, and domineering. Even still, the more I thought about it, I realized what my friend taught his children was not unloving but the exact opposite. He was a tremendous father and his children respected him greatly because he loved them enough to create boundaries and protect them. They knew what to expect because they were disciplined properly.

Similarly, when God created mankind, healthy boundaries (or restrictions) were created to protect Adam from experiencing guilt, shame, and regret. God did not want him to sin, but He gave Adam free will to choose for himself how he would live. The Lord warned Adam that if he ate from the tree of knowledge, death would come upon him. He did not specify which kind of death would result. Adam only knew to avoid that particular tree because God commanded it. No second-guessing was required. Adam did not pull the Lord aside and ask him why such an extreme rule was in effect. He did not feel unfairly judged or restricted from any type of pleasure either. Adam simply listened to God and obeyed His instruction.

There is incredible wisdom in learning obedience, as humility, self-control, and respect for authority are all essential elements. Like baking a cake, the end result will not turn out as it should if we miss one main ingredient. If we pull back on the required amount of flour, sugar, baking powder, or eggs, our cake would not look or taste right. The same holds true for obeying what the Bible teaches. We cannot learn obedience if we are prideful, rebellious, disrespectful, or question God's authority. Rather, we must follow His recipe of righteousness and not deviate from the list of ingredients He requires to sanctify our hearts.

Restriction becomes problematic when we choose to lean on our own understanding rather than God's sovereignty. However, prayer positions us for success when we listen to what the Lord has to say and obey His instructions. Granted, what we believe He says must align with Scripture. If it does, we are left with no other option than to obey His Word without reservation. **"So whoever knows the right thing to do and fails to do it, for him it is sin" (James 4:17)**. The challenge is we have expectations and God's will is not up for debate. For this reason, our personal will must align with His sovereignty, not the opposite.

There have been instances when God laid it on my heart to do something specific and I silenced His voice. Whether it was having a faith discussion, confronting a sin issue, or selflessly serving others in need, I have disobeyed His commands throughout my life. Being uncomfortable was the primary reason I held back due to worldly fear, but I regret those moments. I missed opportunities to be used by Him to bless others. Even persecution could have strengthened my faith had I stood unashamed of the Gospel and boldly defended the Bible as absolute truth. Nevertheless, I ran away from obeying the Lord because all I was concerned about was me.

There is a distinct difference between taking it upon ourselves to do the right thing and disobeying a command. For instance, soldiers are trained to achieve a clear objective on the battlefield. They are expected to follow direct commands and not deviate, but the minor details of how they get from point 'A' to point 'B' are fluid. As long as they work within the boundaries of their training, they will not only minimize their risk of endangerment but protect the lives of those serving alongside them. They will also maximize the likelihood of reaching their objective on time with minimal casualties.

In the Christian church, we follow the same objective. Jesus said, **"Go therefore and make disciples of all nations, baptizing them in the name of the Father and of the Son and of the Holy Spirit, teaching them to observe all that I have commanded you. And behold, I am with you always, to the end of the age"** **(Matthew 28:19–20)**. Placing restrictions on God by picking and choosing whether we will obey His command is foolish, for His Word is not merely an elective in our faith education but the primary objective we must obey wholeheartedly.

At times, God may give us a direct command to speak or act at a specific moment in time. Conversely, He may leave the when and how to our discretion. Nevertheless, our objective is still the same. We must be a light for the kingdom and spread the Good News of Jesus Christ to all nations. Satan wants nothing more than to restrict the power of the Holy Spirit at work in our lives, but we cannot take the bait. God has mighty plans for us, but we must surrender to His authority, obey His Word, and submit to His sovereign will if we want to succeed. Only then will we reach our objective as born-again Christ-followers to the glory of His name.

Application

1. What boundaries have you implemented in your life to protect you from yielding to temptation?

2. Have boundaries been a burden, nuisance, or blessing to your faith journey? How so?

3. Do you feel restricted by God from partaking in the pleasures of this world? Why or why not?

4. How have you restricted yourself from leaning on the wisdom of God in favor of personal experience and intuition?

5. Give an example of a direct command you disobeyed that God gave you in prayer. What did you learn from that experience?

6. In what ways have you restricted God's calling on your life to fulfill the Great Commission and pray for the lost?

7. What has been Satan's greatest tactic to restrict your obedience to God's Word and the discipline of prayer?

Prayer

Lord, I am not as obedient to Your Word as I prefer. There are times when I know You are speaking directly to me with specific instructions on what You want me to do. Oftentimes, I brush aside Your voice and act as if I did not hear You. Please forgive my pride. The opportunities I have missed to serve others in Your name are countless. I have allowed fear to dictate my behavior and my faith feels stagnant because I've been so calloused to the needs of others. Help me obey Your commands with a joyful heart and a genuine desire to honor Your Word so I do not sin against You. Amen.

Day 32 – Vulnerability
Remedy: Search me and know my heart.

"Search me, O God, and know my heart! Try me and know
my thoughts! See if there be any grievous way in me
and lead me in the way everlasting!"

— Psalm 139:23–24 —

Tearing down the walls of vulnerability in our lives is where the rubber meets the road. We can commit to opening up more and allowing others access to our hearts, but oftentimes it is easier said than done. A chasm exists between taking a risk and clinging to safety. For example, there is a huge difference between swimming in the shallow waters of transparency and diving into the deep abyss of vulnerability. Most of us have no construct of what it feels like to bear our souls to others. We would rather hold our cards close and play it safe by controlling the narrative and guarding what information is shared about us, both publicly and privately.

Many people do not know the difference between transparency and vulnerability. Being transparent means we share information about ourselves to the extent we feel comfortable. It does not mean we fail to see the benefits of opening up. Most of us are willing to put some skin in the game and admit our shortcomings and failures. Keep in mind, transparency is healthy, but it pales in comparison to vulnerability where the stakes are higher. When we are vulnerable, we are willing to step over the guardrail and disclose details about ourselves which may change people's perception of us. As a result, anxiety heightens in a vulnerable environment because we do not know what to expect when we air our dirty laundry.

For some, opening up to others is a line they will never cross. For others, they are too scared to talk openly, even with the Lord. What we often fail to realize is that we have nothing to fear because God already knows our thoughts and feelings. Why then do we hold back and play it safe when we pray? Who or what are we protecting other than our pride? God is not shocked by anything we have done nor is He surprised by our thoughts either. What He wants is for us to trust Him and not worry about things which fuel our anxiety. From His perspective, He can turn ashes to beauty at any time. What He needs from us in prayer is full honesty and a willingness to lower our guard.

Psalm 139:23-24 is such an encouragement to our souls. It is the epitome of surrender and holding nothing back. David knew the only way to be sanctified and redeemed was by asking God to convict his heart and reveal his blind spots. His desire to change was pure, so he offered his heart and soul as a humble sacrifice to be cleansed of his sins. What that means for us is simple. When we step into the light and out of the shadows which haunts our minds, we begin the process of reconciliation with our Father in heaven. In other words, we are not scared of getting caught but are focused on obeying the Lord's instruction to live for righteousness.

I can attest that God has humbled me throughout my life and for good reason. I was an extremely stubborn man who would not relent complete control because I thought I knew better. I would play it safe in spiritual settings because I mastered being transparent and knew how to manipulate others into believing I was a righteous man. That is why **"Attributes of a Godly Man"** is such a personal book to me. When I reflect upon it, I am reminded of who I was apart from Christ and how that shaped who I am today. What changed it all was vulnerability. For when I finally lowered my guard and asked the Lord for help, He made a way for me to confess my sins and own the consequences of my actions.

I had to learn how to walk in the light and not hide in the shadows of secrecy. God held me close in those days until I learned to crawl, walk, and run on my own. Today, I plead with men I counsel to open their hearts and take a risk on God just as I did—to share their thoughts and allow the Spirit to reveal what needs to be reconciled. It can be frightening taking a risk. I know the fear and trepidation all too well. Most men have never been taught to talk about their problems. In my opinion, it is the main reason why many wives get frustrated and angry with their husbands. In general, most men are too scared to share their deepest thoughts and expose the depths of their depravity.

Despite our hesitancy, God wants us to push through the ceiling of discomfort and find a way to open up to Him. Prayer is by far the best way to start that process and it begins with owning our failures, confessing our sins, and leaving no stone unturned. When we stop and recognize how our sins nailed Jesus to the cross, we demonstrate that we understand the gravity of our choices. They do not merely have physical or emotional implications but spiritual consequences which far exceed what we expect.

In turn, we must apply the wisdom of Psalm 139:23-24 and allow the Lord unrestricted access to our hearts. Again, He already knows everything about us, so vulnerability is all about reconciling our demons once and for all. The scarlet letter of guilt, shame, and regret can be crippling to bear. It does not benefit us in any way but only drives us deeper into isolation. Therefore, if we want to experience freedom, we must cast off the weight of iniquity and exchange our slavery to sin for the yoke of Jesus Christ which has the power to destroy strongholds and completely set us free.

Application

1. Have you been a master of transparency throughout your life? Why or why not?

2. Make a list of people with whom you are vulnerable? Why are they allowed direct access to your heart and mind?

3. Do you struggle sharing the depths of your soul when you pray? Why or why not?

4. Are you blunt, honest, and unfiltered when you pray to God, or do you try to clean things up before speaking to Him? Which do you believe He prefers?

5. Why is Psalm 139:23-24 a spiritual marker moment in the life of a Christ-follower? What does it reveal about your faith journey?

6. If God already knows your thoughts, feelings, and actions, why fear the discomfort of being vulnerable with Him in prayer?

7. Why does God want you to guard against being transparent all the time? What risk do you take living one-dimensional?

Prayer

Lord, if I am honest, vulnerability scares me. I feel uneasy about asking You to search me, not because of what You will find but what I will be forced to own and change. There are things from my past I never want to think about again—demons I would rather ignore than remove. I want to believe I am righteous before You, but I know my failures all too well. Help me embrace vulnerability and allow You to push things to the surface that I need to reconcile. I must change my ways and that begins with trusting You. Amen.

Day 33 – Worry

Excuse: I'm anxious about what God might ask of me.

"Now the word of the LORD came to Jonah the son of Amittai, saying, 'Arise, go to Nineveh, that great city, and call out against it, for their evil has come up before me.' But Jonah rose to flee to Tarshish from the presence of the LORD. He went down to Joppa and found a ship going to Tarshish. So he paid the fare and went down into it, to go with them to Tarshish, away from the presence of the LORD."

— Jonah 1:1–3 —

How often do we avoid prayer because we are too scared of what the Lord might ask us to do? Why do we offer our lives as a sacrifice to God if we are not genuinely interested in obeying His Word? Obedience is a key pillar of Christianity. We cannot do as we please and expect God to ignore our selfish behavior. We are solely accountable for our actions and must accept whatever consequences arise as a result. Certainly, we hope God turns a blind eye to our disobedience, but that is not the case. He knows and sees all. Thus, the only ones we are deceiving are ourselves, for He is not a genie in a lamp we call upon to grant our never-ending wishes. He is the sovereign Creator of the universe, not our slave.

The life of Jonah is well known. It is a story of rebellion that ends in redemption and accountability. Jonah was a righteous prophet of God. He upheld Old Testament Law and conveyed truth from the Lord to His people. However, Jonah's life took a dramatic turn when God commanded him to go to the people of Nineveh and encourage them to repent of their wickedness. Keep in mind, Jonah was not sent to the clean-cut suburbs of his day to preach a "feel good" sermon. Instead, he was sent to a filthy and depraved slum to declare judgment on a nation and call sinners to repentance.

That is a detail many of us miss in the life of Jonah. Yes, he was a godly man who had great knowledge of Scripture, but he lacked compassion and empathy for his neighbor. He was more concerned with God raining down fire and brimstone on Nineveh than leading a spiritual revival of repentance. Jonah felt entitled to God's grace and mercy, not those around him who rejected Biblical truth and persecuted his religious lifestyle. It begs the question: Do we love our neighbor as ourselves, or do we categorize our sins as less severe or egregious in God's sight?

Jonah positioned himself as holier than the ones God sent him to visit. His pride and self-righteousness led to a stern rebuke when the Lord relented His decision to destroy Ninevah. Jonah could not wrap his mind around the compassion of God to forgive a wicked nation when they repented of their sins. He was too busy waiting on God to punish the Ninevites to recognize that he was just as guilty of condemnation. He needed forgiveness, grace, and mercy just as much as they did, yet he was too distracted by the speck of dust in the eyes of others to see the blatant log in his own (Matt. 7:3–5).

Like Jonah, we worry all the time about what God might ask us to do. We covet being comfortable and having all the pleasures of this world at our disposal. We prefer not to step outside our comfort zone and walk a mile in the shoes of others we cannot identify with. All we can see are differences rather than the common ground we share as sinners before God. Therefore, we are wise not to distance ourselves from those we deem unworthy of God's grace but must speak truth in love to those who desperately need salvation. For **"as it is written: 'None is righteous, no, not one'" (Romans 3:10)**.

Far too often, we worry about the future and miss out on golden opportunities to share the Gospel of Jesus Christ to a lost and broken world. Our testimonies of faith are more than enough to prove that God rescues and redeems the worst of sinners of whom we are living proof. **"I have not come to call the righteous but sinners to repentance" (Luke 5:32).** However, the minute we ignore the Lord's calling to fulfill His Great Commission is the day we should weep and mourn over our sins. God expects us to accept the calling He places on our lives, not avoid them out of fear and trepidation.

Worrying about what God might ask us to do when we pray is a sign of how shortsighted we have become. Like muscle tissue being torn to strengthen it, God is waiting for us to embrace sanctification, not avoid it. We will never grow to our full potential if we are always playing it safe and not putting ourselves in unique positions to be spiritually disciplined. Praying for God to use us as He sees fit can be a frightening, open-ended proposition. We have no idea what He might ask us to do or which direction He might lead us. Nevertheless, if we believe He never leaves or forsakes us, we have complete assurance that His Spirit will guide our path as we fulfill His Great Commission.

The more I allow God to use me as salt and light in a dark world, uncomfortable situations will inevitably follow. In the past, when I have made naïve statements such as never doing something or going somewhere, God has put me in scenarios where I was forced to eat my words. Granted, I have not always understood His sovereignty, but He has proven Himself faithful time and again. I can trust Him no matter what the future holds, even if it makes me feel slightly uncomfortable. Therefore, I will pray for opportunities to be used for His glory because His ways are always better than mine and He knows what I need to become more holy each day.

Application

1. What are you worried about? Why do you fear being stretched beyond your comfort zone?

2. Why is opening your heart to opportunities for ministry one of the scariest aspects of being a Christian?

3. When God prompts you by His Spirit to obey Him in a unique and specific manner, how do you typically respond?

4. Give an example of a time when God gave you a command (like Jonah) and you disobeyed? What did you learn as a result?

5. Why can obedience be so difficult at times in your faith journey? What causes you to run away from the Lord?

6. How have you experienced God's redemption when you chose to obey His will rather than your own?

7. Do you believe the plans God has for you (Jer. 29:11)? Why or why not?

Prayer

Lord, You died on the cross for my sins and that is more than enough reason for me to offer my life to You unconditionally. Why then do I run and hide from obeying Your commands? I am far too concerned about what others might think of me that I ignore Your voice or avoid it altogether by not praying. Please forgive me for taking my salvation for granted. You are far more faithful than I deserve. I repent of my selfish worry. Give me a new heart so I may boldly proclaim Your Gospel to others rather than hide the Good News of Your grace and mercy out of fear of man. Amen.

Day 34 – Discernment

Remedy: God's Word is living and active.

"For the word of God is living and active, sharper than any two-edged sword, piercing to the division of soul and of spirit, of joints and of marrow, and discerning the thoughts and intentions of the heart."

— Hebrews 4:12 —

What does God have to say? That is a question we should ask ourselves in every situation. The problem is that we naturally default to our own understanding when the answers we are looking for are well within our grasp. All we must do is open Scripture and wisdom is readily available for our consumption. The real question is whether we want to know what God thinks or how He calls us to live. In theory, it is easy to declare His Word as our standard of truth, but do our actions prove otherwise? For when culture stretches the definition of what is right and wrong and tempts us to deviate from what the Lord teaches, how will we respond?

When I think about instances where I have been consumed by worry and overwhelmed with anxiety, rarely has my gut reaction been to first open God's Word before moving forward. I often default to figuring things out on my own and exhausting every possible option before praying to God. In many ways, I am far too confident in my ability to know the right thing to do. I think more highly of myself than I ought which usually gets me in trouble. Even so, a deeper issue exists which far surpasses my self-confident attitude. In essence, am I willing to apply what the Bible teaches, unconditionally and without reservation, and pray for wisdom and discernment?

Hebrews 4:12 is where God holds us accountable to the absolute truth of Scripture. It provides the reason why we bristle at Biblical teaching and struggle owning our sins. Oftentimes, we do not want to hear what God has to say because His Word forces us to examine our lives and make changes. Conviction cuts like a knife and draws a clear line between black and white (right and wrong). Conversely, grey is more comfortable and easily adaptable. We can manipulate it to conform to any situation, which is why we prefer to lean on our own understanding or naïve interpretation of Scripture rather than what it plainly states in black and white.

Unfortunately, many in the church today do not believe the Bible is absolute truth cover-to-cover. We want Jesus to be our Savior but not our Lord, because lordship forces us to relinquish our rights and align our personal will with His righteous law. That is often why we struggle distinguishing light from darkness. Nevertheless, would it not be important to know where the cliff's edge is to avoid falling? Are we so foolish as to not pray for wisdom? Our arrogance speaks to the justifying nature of the flesh which desires worldly pleasures without consequences. We crave the best of both worlds, yet God's Word draws a line in the sand to distinguish right from wrong.

The beauty of having an absolute standard of righteousness is that we can discern God's will more easily. We are not left guessing what He believes because His Word is clear. Some of the biggest and most controversial social issues of our day are black and white from Scripture's standpoint. Ambiguity is not an option, yet there is incredible confusion in the church. The problem is that social issues are deeply personal. We feel unloving or judgmental if we take a moral stand against someone's free will to discern their own path, but are we not liable on judgment day if we do not warn them of the dangers of disobeying God's command?

Prayerful discernment is a critical part of our daily lives. We have far too many decisions to make which require careful consideration. Therefore, prayer (and not personal experience) is our gateway to discernment. In so many ways, we need God's wisdom because our knowledge is limited. As such, we must humble ourselves and lean upon the Lord who can safely guide our paths. **"If any of you lacks wisdom, let him ask God, who gives generously to all without reproach, and it will be given him. But let him ask in faith, with no doubting, for the one who doubts is like a wave of the sea that is driven and tossed by the wind" (James 1:5–6).**

Scripture affirms that God is our ultimate source of truth, but we must ask Him by faith to reveal His wisdom when we pray. Otherwise, we will doubt whether His Word is true. Faith is the true foundation of discernment. When we yield to God's omniscience, we are guaranteed protection from the enemy's snare. That does not mean harm will pass us by if we align with Scripture. The joy of our salvation in Christ is secure for eternity regardless of the afflictions we experience this side of heaven. It reassures that He will never leave or forsake us no matter what trials we face. Thus, our faith in the power and validity of His Word cannot waver.

Proper discernment is critical to survival. We will never know the best course of action to choose if we are not leaning upon the Lord for wisdom. That does not mean accepting what He has to say will be easy. When we pray for wisdom, we must prepare our hearts to receive hard truth which will challenge us to deviate from the world. For when we relinquish our personal rights and yield to the lordship of Christ, we are guaranteed that He will fight our battles. We need not fear the enemy because **"the word of the Lord lasts forever" (1 Peter 1:25)**, so let us trust in His wisdom and not waver when Satan unleashes his relentless attack against us.

Application

1. How often do you ask yourself, "What does God have to say?" How can that question compel you to pray more?

2. Who or what do you lean on when making decisions to discern the wisest course of action? Why?

3. Where does God's Word fall in your hierarchy of trusted people or resources you seek when consumed by worry?

4. Give an example of a moral principle God expects you to align with as a Christian. What does His Word say? What worries you about defending what the Bible teaches?

5. Why is Hebrews 4:12 so convicting? How has God proven this promise to be true in your life?

6. How often do you pray for wisdom and discernment? Do you believe it is sufficient? Why or why not?

7. Is proper discernment possible outside of God's Word? Why or why not?

Prayer

Lord, I worry so much about what I should say or do in life that I often forget to stop and pray for wisdom. Your Word is a lamp to my feet and a light to my path, yet I fail to read it daily. Help me not to lean on my own understanding for wisdom but read Your Word instead. Everything that pertains to life and godliness is found in its pages, so help me to never waver when trusting the inerrancy of Scripture. I need not fear the enemy so long as my faith, hope, and trust are in the saving power of Your Word. Amen.

Day 35 – Frustration

Excuse: God didn't answer how I wanted.

"What causes quarrels and what causes fights among you?
Is it not this, that your passions are at war within you?
You desire and do not have, so you murder. You covet and
cannot obtain, so you fight and quarrel. You do not have,
because you do not ask. You ask and do not receive,
because you ask wrongly, to spend it on your passions."

— James 4:1–3 —

Why do we get frustrated when the Lord answers our prayers but not in the time or manner we expect? Do we have any right to voice our displeasure or must we silence our opinion and accept the hand we've been dealt? Frustration is a powerful emotion to consider. On the one hand, it can be extremely dangerous if we allow it to drive a wedge in our relationship with the Lord. On the other hand, we have plenty of examples in the book of Psalms where King David wore his emotions on his sleeve and held nothing back. He voiced his displeasure to God on numerous occasions and committed no sin in doing so. Why then should we be concerned with holding back how we feel when we pray?

For better or worse, frustration seems to make its way into many of our prayers. When we look around and see the world spiraling out of control, we can easily get irritated and wonder, "Why is God not intervening?" The political landscape in which we live is enough to make our blood boil when morality is not only suppressed but persecuted. In many ways, our culture is far more concerned with silencing Biblical truth (when we hold firm to its precepts) than hearing what God has to say and considering His position. What are we to do? How should we respond? Are we allowed to succumb to emotion and express our frustrations to the Lord without sinning?

God always answers prayer. We may not recognize when or how, but He guides our path to ensure all things work together for our good, whether we realize it or not. Keep in mind, He never guarantees prosperity according to worldly riches. Rather, He reminds us of our hope in Christ which provides eternal perspective and blesses us infinitely. Think about how difficult trials would be without the Holy Spirit guarding our hearts and guiding our path. We would be hopelessly lost without the Lord's wisdom and discernment. For **"the joy of the Lord is our strength" (Nehemiah 8:10)**, and in Him we find rest for our tired and weary souls.

When I consider how easily I complain to God in prayer, I am convicted. My mind is often consumed with the pains of inconvenience rather than the blessings of sanctification. Gaining knowledge and receiving wisdom is often supplanted by negative attitudes that do nothing but stunt my spiritual growth. It is quite embarrassing to look in the mirror and see how tunnel-visioned I am on my own well-being. I am quick to vent frustrations when things do not turn out how I think they should because I am more concerned about myself than anyone else.

Perhaps if I opened my Bible more frequently, I would realize that God did not promise me ease and comfort in this broken world but trials which test the depth and breadth of my faith. Jesus said, **"In the world you will have tribulation. But take heart; I have overcome the world" (John 16:33)**. Why then would I ever doubt His sovereignty which puts me in positions where my faith is tested? The true measure of faith is not based upon how I respond when life is prosperous but rather on how I react when Satan has dismantled or destroyed all that I hold dear. As a result, I must not yield to frustration but trust the Lord to protect me, come what may.

I can attest that inconvenience is the #1 reason I get frustrated. When others fail to listen to my perspective or heed my advice, I feel slighted. When personal outcomes differ from what I hoped for or expected, I voice my displeasure. If the world does not revolve around my personal preferences, frustration boils to the surface. Eventually, what is locked up inside comes bursting forth when enough pressure is exerted against my psyche. If my attitude is poor, criticism and complaining overwhelm my focus and spread like a deadly virus, promoting further destruction.

We must remember that the world does not revolve around us, and neither does God for that matter. No matter the reason, frustration cannot become the bedrock of our communication with God. He will certainly allow us ample opportunity to release all we are thinking and feeling in prayer. Even still, once our emotions are purged, we must return to center and guard our hearts moving forward. There are times when it is good to cast our cares upon the Lord, no matter how raw, honest, or vulnerable they may be. Trials tend to expose what is bottled up inside of us, which means we must express our hearts to God to avoid falling prey to frustration.

James 4:1-3 reminds us that our greatest battle is overcoming the urge to yield to our feelings and allow emotions to guide us. We also cannot hold the Lord hostage to do our bidding or else. Only a fool would be so naïve as to place expectations upon Him. We are not the center of the universe by any means, for **"whatever the LORD pleases, he does, in heaven and on earth, in the seas and all deeps" (Psalm 135:6)**. God longs to hear what is on our hearts and minds but we must release our emotions and move on, for slavery comes to those who allow frustration to consume their psyche and become their stronghold.

Application

1. How easily do you get frustrated when things fail to work out the way you think they should?

2. When you pray, is God more apt to hear praise and worship or complaining and frustration? Why?

3. What frustrates you more than anything in this world? How so?

4. Why is it so easy to identify things you are frustrated about than pray to God and rectify them in a healthy manner?

5. How do you typically talk to God in prayer? Is frustration a part of your daily communication? Why or why not?

6. What role does inconvenience play in fueling your frustrations?

7. Does frustration control you more than you control it? How so?

8. How can you avoid placing expectations upon God to do your bidding? What needs to change in your prayers?

Prayer

Lord, thank You for saving me. You died for my sins so I could be rescued from the pattern of this world and redeemed by Your grace. For far too long, I have been enslaved to emotions. When trouble comes, I vent my frustrations without ever considering how they poison my attitude. I never want to be known as someone who people avoid because all I do is complain about what is bothering me. I know that You see the error of my ways but help me hear Your Spirit's conviction more clearly. I repent of the unrealistic expectations I have placed upon You. You are always gracious to me and I thank You for loving me despite my frustrations. Amen.

Day 36 – Contentment
Remedy: The Lord has done great things.

"The LORD has done great things for us; we are glad."

— *Psalm 126:3* —

Contentment is a powerful tool in the life of a Christ-follower. It can be the difference between success and failure, triumph, or frustration. When we are tempted to throw in the towel and give up hope for a brighter tomorrow, contentment reminds us that God is sovereignly in control despite our circumstances. No matter how bleak the future might seem, the Lord knows exactly what lies ahead and will ensure our needs are met at all times. All we must do is trust His plan and remain content despite what we assume we need to survive. **"For the sake of Christ, then, I am content with weaknesses, insults, hardships, persecutions, and calamities. For when I am weak, then I am strong" (2 Corinthians 12:10).**

Contentment is arguably the key to living a happy and peaceful life. It compels us to appreciate what the Lord has given rather than focusing attention on what we lack. It helps us count our blessings and not get frustrated with God, thus demanding things which are irrelevant. Paul understood the difference between survival needs and the pleasures of this world which are non-essential. He warned us not to be consumed by fleeting treasures that will never satisfy but godly character which guards our hearts and minds against discontentment. **"But godliness with contentment is great gain, for we brought nothing into the world, and we cannot take anything out of the world. But if we have food and clothing, with these we will be content" (1 Timothy 6:6–8).**

Discontentment towards God arises when answers to prayer do not come in the time or manner we expect. We accuse Him of mistrust because He leads us down paths we never would have chosen for ourselves. As a result, we question whether prayer is even worth the effort if frustration is all we receive in return. What we need is a healthy dose of perspective, grounded in the reality of all God has done for us. In other words, we must shift our perspective from glass-half-empty to glass-half-full. In turn, we will give thanks for all the blessings the Lord provides rather than wallow in the shadows of shame, regret, and despair.

Becoming embittered by frustration is a recipe for giving up on prayer. We cannot allow Satan to occupy the high ground where he can pick us off like a long-range sniper. We must level the battlefield, which begins with not surrendering our shield of faith, helmet of salvation, or sword of the Spirit to the enemy. Rather, we must put on the full armor of God which is bathed in unending prayer to our Lord and Savior. Satan knows if he can get us to abandon prayer, our communication line to God is severed. Like a soldier losing all radio contact to central command, we are left vulnerable to attack when we abandon prayer out of frustration or discontentment.

When I reflect upon the years I struggled with sexual sin, I am reminded of how often I prayed that God would rescue me from temptation. I envied those who walked away from addiction and quit cold turkey, so I asked God to give me strength to do likewise. I figured that was the key to overcoming sin, so I waited for Him to eliminate my yearning for sexual fulfillment altogether. The problem was I was still a married man and removing desire for my wife was not healthy nor wise. I needed self-control, not abstinence, because discontentment with God's provision was the real problem which plagued my heart and mind.

Unfortunately, what ensued was frustration and bitterness with the Lord's answer to my prayers. I preferred that my memory be wiped clean, but He did not give me permanent amnesia from the past nor completely remove sexual desire from my life. Rather, He had me look upon His precious gift of sex as pure and holy. He did not give me the quick fix I coveted. Instead, He taught me to fall in love with my wife again with pure eyes and a steadfast commitment to love her like Christ. The Lord proved to me that contentment was the key to overcoming unmet expectations and achieving peace in my life and marriage.

It is amazing how a fresh perspective can open our eyes to things we did not see before. The bounty of God's provision surrounds us daily, yet we fold our arms and pout when we fail to get our way. Why? What makes us assume we know what is best at all times? Scripture reminds us, **"The eyes of the Lord are in every place, keeping watch on the evil and the good" (Proverbs 15:3)**. We need not worry whether He has our best interests in mind. The Lord is not surprised by anything. He knows the desires and intentions of our hearts and answers our prayers as He sees fit according to His omniscience.

That does not mean contentment is easy to achieve. Incredible self-control is required to not covet the pleasures of this world but remain satisfied with what we have. Therefore, we must take stock of our lives before we come to the Lord in prayer and count our blessings, because He has done great things for us. Contentment is not about brainwashing ourselves into assuming everything is okay when clearly it is not. It simply means that we trust God with our lives and not yield to bitterness when we do not get what we want. The more we appreciate God's provision rather than question it, the happier and more content we will be with His sovereignty.

Application

1. How would you define contentment? What does it look like from a practical perspective?

2. Why does contentment depend upon a proper understanding of God's sovereignty?

3. If "godliness with contentment is great gain" (1 Tim. 6:6), how can you pray for and possess more godly character?

4. What do you have to be thankful for today? How has the Lord blessed you beyond measure?

5. Why do you allow Satan to cut-off your communication line to God in prayer? How have you given the enemy the high ground?

6. Have you become embittered by frustration over unmet desires and unanswered prayers? How so?

7. Why is it critical to always be content with what you have (God's provision) but never content with who you are (sanctification)?

Prayer

Lord, Your grace and mercy are new every morning. Thank You for giving me new life in Christ and leading me away from the pleasures of this fallen world. Your sovereign provision is perfect. Help me to never forget the sacrifice You made for the forgiveness of my sins. I am often distracted by what I think I need to be happy and get frustrated when things fail to work out how I think they should. I realize that my knowledge is limited, but please give me wisdom to trust You with all my heart. I long to walk in the light of contentment, fully satisfied by Your grace and truth. Amen.

Day 37 – Embarrassment
Excuse: My prayers are too immature.

"But Moses said to the LORD, 'Oh, my Lord, I am not eloquent,
either in the past or since you have spoken to your servant, but I am
slow of speech and of tongue.' Then the LORD said to him,
'Who has made man's mouth? Who makes him mute, or deaf,
or seeing, or blind? Is it not I, the LORD? Now therefore go,
and I will be with your mouth and teach you what you shall speak.'"

— Exodus 4:10–12 —

Why do we become so embarrassed in our faith journey? For instance, the moment we witness someone pray aloud who is eloquent of speech and tongue, we question whether we are doing it right. Envy takes root in our hearts and we wonder why we do not pray better, even though the Lord is far less concerned with the words of our mouth than the meditations of our heart. For this reason, Jesus taught His disciples to pray as such: **"And when you pray, do not heap up empty phrases as the Gentiles do, for they think that they will be heard for their many words. Do not be like them, for your Father knows what you need before you ask him"** (Matthew 6:7–8).

What Jesus sought to engrain in the minds of His followers was that the sacrifices of God are a broken spirit. It is no different than the parable of the Pharisee and the tax collector (Luke 18:9-14), which Jesus used to illustrate a point about the posture and condition of our hearts before God in heaven. The key to effective prayer begins with reverence. No man, woman, or child can expect to stand righteous before the throne of grace in their own human strength. We must be cleansed and forgiven—washed by the blood of the Lamb for the forgiveness of sins. The only thing that matters when we lift our eyes to heaven is genuine acknowledgment of our emptiness apart from the Lord's provision.

The moment we realize that nothing can separate us from the love of Christ, our lives will never be the same. We no longer have to live in fear of man or be ashamed of our past, because Jesus paid it all to set us free. Embarrassment is nothing but a tool of the devil to enslave us to covetousness and insecurity. The enemy baits us into thinking we need to be like those we assume are holier than us for our prayers to be answered. However, comparison can easily become a bottleneck in our journey of faith if we are chasing idols which have no bearing on God's heart.

In Exodus 4:10-12, Moses had doubts about his ability to stand before Pharoah and speak on the Lord's behalf. He attempted to sway God's calling with reasons about why he was unqualified. His insecurity with public speaking is not uncommon. In many ways, we think we need to speak more eloquently for the Lord to hear our prayers. Unfortunately, we miss the point entirely because He uses broken vessels to do His will far more than the spiritual elite. Reason being, it takes a sinner to know one, and those willing to bear their souls and share their personal testimonies have the power to fulfill the Great Commission in ways others cannot.

I have spent two-thirds of my life working in sales. My first real job was selling vacuum cleaners door-to-door. I spent the last three years of college selling hot tubs as a commission salesman before jumping into corporate sales for the past twenty-five years. I have excelled in singing and acting and spent a considerable amount of time on stage performing for large audiences. If anyone should be comfortable standing up and speaking publicly, it should be me, yet I get nervous and wrestle with insecurity like everyone else.

Unfortunately, I have struggled with embarrassment in prayer for the majority of my life. My wife has heard me complain frequently about feeling immature and inadequate as a spiritual leader. I have been insecure about my ability to pray for far too long but also spent little time remedying the issue. As such, I cannot sit and complain about feeling like a spiritual baby if I am unwilling to stop crawling and start walking on my own. My embarrassment is simply a figment of my imagination than reality itself, for God is not concerned about the eloquence of my prayers. As a result, it is time I stop assuming that I need to be someone other than who God made me and start opening my heart to Him on a regular basis.

When we read the Psalms, we should be encouraged that David did not care about what others thought of him. His only concern was remaining true to his faith and bearing his soul before the Lord at all times. Scripture refers to him as a man after God's own heart, and we should learn from his example and not stress about what others may think of our prayers. God knows the intentions of our hearts and will accept our petitions as long as we are humble and reverent. **"The sacrifices of God are a broken spirit; a broken and contrite heart, O God, you will not despise" (Psalm 51:17).**

The worst thing we could ever do is abandon prayer because we believe the meditations of our hearts are juvenile. Spiritual immaturity is all about not knowing what to do but trying to figure it out apart from the Lord's help. That is not what God desires, though. Scripture affirms that He will accept our humble petitions no matter how simple or raw our words may be. Sometimes, we do not know what to say. However, we know the Spirit intercedes on our behalf (Rom. 8:26). It is a beautiful gift because it means the fluency of our speech is inconsequential. All that truly matters is our posture before our Lord which must remain humble and reverent.

Application

1. Do you struggle with embarrassment when you pray? Why or why not?

2. How has Satan used comparison to make you doubt whether you are praying correctly?

3. What do you believe is the most important aspect of effective prayer? Why?

4. How has embarrassment caused covetousness and insecurity in your prayer life?

5. Do you believe you need to be someone you are not for God to hear your prayers? Why or why not?

6. Why is embarrassment more often a figment of your imagination than true reality?

7. Why is spiritual immaturity more about pride than anything else?

Prayer

Lord, I am ashamed to admit I have allowed personal insecurity to become a bottleneck in my relationship with You. Nothing in Your Word tells me that I need to clean up my act before coming to You in repentance. All You are concerned about is the condition of my heart, not the eloquence of my speech. Help me guard my mind against comparison. I have nothing to be embarrassed about when I pour out my heart in prayer. Help me to also drown out the enemy's noise which tempts me to give up praying. For I know my prayers are not immature in Your sight but honest, and I humbly thank You for always hearing them. Amen.

Day 38 – Innocence
Remedy: Come like children into the kingdom.

*"Jesus said, 'Truly, I say to you, unless you turn and become
like children, you will never enter the kingdom of heaven.
Whoever humbles himself like this child is the greatest
in the kingdom of heaven.'"*

— Matthew 18:3–4 —

The last thing we tend to think about when we approach God in prayer is our spiritual innocence. Granted, we may struggle reconciling how guilty we feel for sins we have committed, but that is not the essence of what it means to come to the Lord as blameless. Childlike innocence is the epitome of what God expects when we approach His throne of grace. He does not want us to think more highly of ourselves than we ought but to come to Him with love and trust as we seek His favor and approval. As our heavenly Father, He longs to care for all our needs but expects us to approach Him in humility as well.

Those of us who are parents understand this reality completely. Not a day goes by when our children are not eager to tell us all that is on their minds as they beg for our attention. They are determined to provide a detailed report of their day because they desire to see our reaction and receive affirmation. They desire love and affection and crave encouragement constantly. They are dependent upon our physical protection, but even more on our emotional, psychological, and spiritual provision as well. In turn, God holds us accountable to raise them in the discipline and instruction of His Word (Eph. 6:4), for they are precious in His sight.

Similarly, we are expected to run to our heavenly Father and share all that is on our hearts. We need not feel embarrassed nor hesitant, assuming we are too old or mature to come to God in such a way. Instead, He wants us to be our true and authentic selves, not concerned with what others may think of us. The only opinion that matters is His, for He shaped us in His image so we could have a personal relationship with His Son, Jesus Christ. **"For you formed my inward parts; you knitted me together in my mother's womb. I praise you, for I am fearfully and wonderfully made. Wonderful are your works; my soul knows it very well" (Psalm 139:13–14).**

I do not know why, but I have always struggled with coming to the Father like a little child. I am convinced that pride is at the core of my discomfort. Reason being, I want to be on a level playing field with the Lord and have a mature conversation, or so I think. Being childish feels wrong, yet I know that is not the essence of what Jesus taught in Matthew 18:3-4. God wants a relationship with me where I can humble myself and come to Him daily. Therefore, I must step out of the shadows of isolation and allow Him access to the deepest corners of my heart. He longs to free me from bondage, but it is ultimately my choice whether I allow Him to save me.

It seems quite arrogant to assume that coming to the Father like a child is somehow a sign of weakness. Children trust completely. They have no reason to doubt their parent's love until they are given one. Oftentimes, we cast our insecurities upon God and judge Him based on the pain and disappointment we experienced growing up. We tend to remember all the broken promises our parents made to us and assume God is no different. However, He is far greater than we could ever imagine, for His love is everlasting, pure, and withstands the test of time.

Keep in mind, we cannot filter the Lord through our behavioral lens because sinful man is selfish and flawed. God does not operate in ways we can comprehend. **"For my thoughts are not your thoughts, neither are your ways my ways, declares the LORD. For as the heavens are higher than the earth, so are my ways higher than your ways and my thoughts than your thoughts" (Isaiah 55:8–9)**. Rather, He sees what we cannot. So, our posture before Him must be compelled by unwavering hope and trust that He knows what we need long before we do, for He will bring all things to fruition in due time.

We need not fear the terror of the night nor the arrow that flies by day because the Lord holds the whole world in the palm of His hands. All He expects from us in return is a commitment to open our hearts and not close ourselves off from the power of His love and forgiveness. The blessings which await those who humble themselves like little children at the feet of Jesus is immeasurable. Our attitude improves when we realize that we have nothing to worry about. Fear and doubt drift away as we relinquish our pride and insecurities, for the enemy is powerless to harm us when we rest in the arms of Christ.

Truly, we are called to set aside embarrassment and come to the Lord like innocent children, because we are loved more than we realize. Surrendering our hearts to God is the essence of humility which begins with not thinking more highly of ourselves than we ought. Prayer is all about developing a deeper relationship with God, but that cannot come to fruition if we are unwilling to humble ourselves and admit how desperately we need Him. We must embrace our dependance upon Jesus and resist isolating ourselves further, because joy and peace come to those who enter the kingdom of heaven like innocent children.

Application

1. What does it mean to come to the Father like a little child?

2. Why is childlike innocence so important to developing a personal relationship with God?

3. Why do children love, hope, and trust so easily? What can you learn from their example?

4. Do you believe that childlike innocence is a sign of weakness or strength? How so?

5. How could your prayer life benefit if you came to Jesus each day solely dependent upon His provision and not your own?

6. How has your relationship with your earthly father impacted the relationship you have with the Lord?

7. Are you willing to be 100% dependent on God to meet all your needs? Why or why not?

Prayer

Lord, when I think about what it means to come to You like a little child, I am encouraged. A great weight is lifted off my shoulders because I no longer have to concern myself with assuming I need to be perfect. I can come to You just as I am without guilt, shame, or embarrassment. Thank You for accepting me despite the immaturity of my prayers. I cannot begin to express how blessed I am by Your sovereign provision. You embrace me despite my faults and hear my prayers even when I cannot find words to express how I feel. Thank You for loving me and calling me Your beloved child. Your grace and mercy are indescribable, Lord! Amen.

Day 39 – Bitterness
Excuse: Why did God abandon me?

*"See to it that no one fails to obtain the grace of God;
that no 'root of bitterness' springs up and causes trouble,
and by it many become defiled."*

— *Hebrews 12:15* —

Perhaps the greatest challenge to developing a healthy prayer life occurs at the crossroads of bitterness. Not a day goes by where the enemy does not tempt us to abandon our faith and yield to fleshly desires. When life does not turn out how we presume, or our prayers are not answered according to our personal preferences, we feel justified holding God accountable and judging Him for His response. A root of bitterness begins to develop when we point a finger at the Lord and blame Him for our plight. Before we know it, we can reach an unfortunate verdict that He is to blame for our misery and vow to never lean upon Him again in times of need.

Bitterness is a powerful tool for creating division and dissension. Satan knows how to wield a sword and cut off our prayer line to the Father. He knows how vulnerable we are to unmet expectations, so he tempts us to assume our petitions to God are more than reasonable to set us up for disappointment. One of his most effective tactics centers on what we would consider righteous prayers. For instance, when someone we love is faced with a grave health diagnosis, it is not only right to pray for healing but to also trust that God can bring healing to fruition. However, the minute we place expectations that He absolutely will bring healing, we set ourselves up for failure and allow a seed of bitterness to take root in our hearts.

There is nothing wrong with righteous prayers. Where we get off track is judging the goodness of God based upon how He responds. Obviously, we are not God. His ways are higher and He sees what we cannot. Moreover, His purposes exceed the depth and breadth of human understanding. If He chooses to go one way vs. another, it is completely at His discretion to do so because He is sovereign. Nothing happens outside the realm of His omniscience because we go no place by accident. In turn, our personal experiences are ordained with specific purposes and intentions which we cannot truly comprehend in the moment.

I have seen this situation play out in the life of one of my closest friends. He is a dear brother in Christ I love wholeheartedly, but he was blindsided one day when his granddaughter was born with a rare birth defect. To say He was devastated by the news was a gross understatement, but his faith in Christ compelled him to turn to the Lord and pray for her healing. Months passed with countless doctor appointments and surgical procedures. Things would improve and then come crashing down with frustration and disappointment. He was beginning to exhaust himself being the patriarchal rock of his family, but his faith began showing signs of wear and tear due to fatigue, confusion, misunderstanding, and bitterness.

One night he called me on a long drive home. We chatted a bit and then I began to question him on how he was doing about his granddaughter's condition. At first, he declared that God was going to do a miracle and heal her completely. Yet the more I listened, underneath the surface, he was completely frustrated. He could not comprehend why God would allow this tragedy to happen. If the Lord was indeed good, He would heal her! I could empathize with his confusion but the tone of our conversation immediately turned dark when this righteous man of God broke down in anger and rage.

He did not want to hear me say, "Keep the faith, brother!" What he needed was a verbal punching bag, and I allowed him to pound away at me so he could purge his heart of the bitterness he had been harboring. What I finally encouraged him to do was shift his focus from expectational outcomes to prayers of understanding. In other words, continue to pray for healing, but bind that request with a sincere desire for clarity and understanding if God chooses not to answer in the time or manner he prefers. The minute he did, peace filled his heart and he began to minister to his family with healthy perspective and a renewed trust in God's sovereignty.

Faith is not easy. It takes an incredible amount of courage to step outside our door and face the world with divine purpose, come what may. We are tempted to give in to bitterness the minute things take an unexpected turn. However, those are the moments when we need wisdom and discernment to survive another day. As followers of Christ, we know He is our fountain of wisdom and hope in the face of uncertainty. Only He has the power to save us, but we must lay our burdens down and give Him ample opportunity to meet our needs as He sees fit. That does not mean accepting hardship is easy, but we can endure it better if we have an understanding and healthy perspective in the face of unanswered prayer.

Jesus paid it all so we would never have to worry about pain or suffering for eternity. Nevertheless, while we remain here, we will surely face difficulty and persecution. Satan is relentless in his attack on the saints of God and will stop at nothing until he has cultivated a root of bitterness in our personal relationship with Christ. Thus, we must guard our hearts from expecting specific outcomes in prayer or allow God's response to dictate His goodness. Rather, we must praise Him because He is good despite our struggles and will work things together for our good, even when we fail to see how.

Application

1. What does a root of bitterness look like?

2. Give an example where bitterness took hold of your heart and distanced you from the Lord? What did you learn?

3. Is there any injustice you blame God for in your heart? How has that directly impacted your prayer life?

4. What are the dangers of painting God in a box and praying for specific outcomes?

5. Do you ever pray for wisdom and understanding to accompany your requests to God? Why or why not?

6. How have you allowed bitterness to become a stronghold? How can you lay it at the foot of the cross instead?

7. How have you experienced lasting freedom by accepting God's sovereignty, come what may?

Prayer

Lord, the battleground of my heart is heavy laden with trials which tempt me to turn my back on You. The enemy is determined to convince me that You are not good because the miracles I desire are at Your discretion. You see what I cannot and I confess that I've held a grudge against You for far too long. I often blame You for not hearing my cries for help when that is not true. You are closer to me than a brother. Help me realize how gracious You are despite my difficult circumstances. You have never failed me, Lord, and You never will. Please give me wisdom where I lack understanding and the confidence to trust Your will rather than my own. Amen.

Day 40 – Goodness
Remedy: All things work together for good.

"And we know that for those who love God all things work together for good, for those who are called according to his purpose."

— *Romans 8:28* —

When we are overwhelmed by trials and it feels like the world is crashing down all around us, it can be hard to remember that God is in control. Nothing happens outside of His sovereign will for our lives, whether blessings from above or persecution from the enemy. In all things, the Lord reigns supreme, both now and forever. There are no accidents in His plan for our lives. In turn, we need not worry about the future nor the trials we face each day. There is a divine reason and purpose for everything we experience this side of heaven, which we often cannot understand nor fully comprehend in the moment.

The challenge is that when life becomes difficult, we often turn to the Lord in prayer expecting immediate answers and detailed explanations. We want reprieve from our calamity, yet understanding why we are made to suffer is a tough pill to swallow. It is an incredible test of faith when God remains silent in an hour of great need. We often wonder whether He even hears us because silence is deafening when we pray so hard but our circumstances fail to change. It can tempt us to walk away from our faith in Christ and succumb to bitterness and despair.

The apostle Paul understood this struggle mightily. In his second letter to the Corinthian church, he spoke about a thorn in the flesh which tormented him. Scripture does not detail what the affliction was, but Paul prayed three times for God to relieve his suffering and received an answer he likely did not expect. **"But he said to me, 'My grace is sufficient for you, for my power is made perfect in weakness.' Therefore I will boast all the more gladly of my weaknesses, so that the power of Christ may rest upon me"** (2 Corinthians 12:9).

What Paul learned was a hard lesson we know intimately as well. Not every prayer will be answered in the time or manner we prefer. Sometimes, the Lord will answer, "Yes," but His goodness is not contingent upon meeting our desires. Rather, He determines what is in our best interest which may or may not be what we had hoped. It is difficult to trust God when unmet expectations plague our minds. For this reason, He encourages us to lean not on our own understanding (Prov. 3:5). Our vantage point is limited and we are not afforded the privilege of knowing the future, so we must relinquish control to God and not worry about tomorrow.

My mother was an amazing woman—kind and compassionate, honest, and trustworthy. She was the epitome of a loving wife and mother. Of course, she was not perfect, but in my eyes she was a selfless and incredible woman of God. She passed away over twenty years ago due to cancer at the age of sixty-three. She did have the opportunity to see Amber and I get married but died less than two years later. Regrettably, my four daughters never knew her, which is incredibly tragic. All they have are memories I share and pictures of moments in time which they never knew.

It is difficult to convey what a loss that is for me. When I look at my girls, I see different aspects of my Mom in their demeanor and likeness. She would have loved their unique gifts, personalities, and interests. I can only imagine the joy she would have experienced spending time with my family had the Lord not called her home so young. I struggle understanding why such a gracious, loving, and godly woman never saw her granddaughters grow up. She never had the chance to bless them with her loving kindness. All I know is that she is no longer with us, and I am left with wondering why she is no longer living here on earth.

What I have learned and come to accept is that God is still good despite the pain I feel. It feels counterintuitive to praise Him when all I want to do is weep and mourn, but I know that joy comes in the morning. No matter how much I wonder how it would have been had my mother not died, I cannot allow my heart to blame God for taking her home. She spent the final eighteen months of her life ravaged by cancer. Today, she celebrates pain-free in heaven, glorifying Christ who gave her eternal life. How then could I embitter my heart against the One who healed and saved her?

It takes spiritual maturity and foresight to recognize the goodness of God in pain and sorrow. Scripture affirms, **"Count it all joy, my brothers, when you meet trials of various kinds, for you know that the testing of your faith produces steadfastness" (James 1:2–3)**. There is a purpose for every trial we face which may not be visible in the moment. Therefore, we need hindsight perspective in prayer to comprehend the glory of God's sovereignty and how He works all things for our good, even when we cannot see how.

We can rest peacefully because the Lord sees us in our hour of need and hears us when we pray. To believe otherwise is foolish, because the Lord has a divine purpose for everything we experience in life. In turn, we must guard our hearts from becoming bitter or questioning His goodness. That does not mean trusting God is easy. Rather, it means we know who is ultimately in control and will yield our hearts to His sovereign will rather than our own, for the Lord is good no matter the trials we face in life and death.

Application

1. How can Romans 8:28 transform your prayer life by helping you guard against frustration and bitterness?

2. Do you believe God is in control of all things? Why or why not?

3. How has the Lord proven Himself faithful in your hour of need despite the outcome?

4. Why does God often make you wait patiently rather than answer your prayers immediately?

5. How do you relate to Paul's "thorn in the flesh" dilemma?

6. Do you struggle trusting God when your prayers are left unanswered? Why or why not?

7. Why do you worry about tomorrow when God is sovereign?

8. How can you consider trials as joy and avoid allowing bitterness to sway your belief that God is always good?

Prayer

Lord, no matter how busy You are, You always make time for me and hear my cries for help. Far too often, I expect specific outcomes when I pray and get frustrated and bitter when I do not get my way. Please forgive me. I lack Your knowledge and foresight, and that tends to influence how much I trust You when trials come. Help me to not be swayed by emotion but trust Your Word which affirms that You will never leave or forsake me. I desperately need You in my life and will continue to pray for Your wisdom when I lack understanding. You are so good to me, Lord. Help me to never forget Your faithfulness when trials come my way. Amen.

POSTFACE

Igniting Spiritual Revival

What a journey it has been! When I endeavored to write this devotional, I never envisioned how convicting it would be to expose my fears, doubts, and insecurities regarding prayer. There is something powerful about putting a pen to paper and exposing lies I have chosen to believe. When I reflect upon what God has laid upon my heart, I cannot help but fall on my knees and worship Him. I wasted so many years making excuses for my prayer struggles and perfecting the art of laziness that I put God on hold. I minimized the importance of prayer which only made it easier to justify why I failed to lead my family as a godly role model.

Oftentimes, we forget that the enemy prowls around, waiting for us to lower our guard so he can attack. Concerning prayer, Satan wants to distract us more than anything, which is why all twenty excuses in this book are examples of how he draws our attention away from absolute truth. He wants to keep us enslaved to our sins. Keep in mind, each excuse we studied was countered with a specific remedy to point us toward God's Word as our source of wisdom and clarity. That does mean applying what the Bible teaches is easy. It merely points us in the right direction and demonstrates what it will take to overcome all obstacles and find hope and healing.

Prayer is one of the greatest weaknesses in the church today and rarely do we talk about how to remedy it. We do not care to admit our failures and shortcomings nor confess we struggle finding value praying on a consistent basis. I certainly have been convicted and embarrassed talking about how I treated God as nothing more than a genie in a bottle to grant my wishes. I grieve and mourn the guilt of my confession because He deserves my reverence, not arrogance. I relegated the Creator of the universe to a puppet, expecting Him to give me what I wanted. For that, I am incredibly remorseful.

Pride and arrogance are not things we often talk about in church, yet we struggle with them deep in our hearts. How then do we remedy the problem? Keep in mind, this devotional was not meant to enslave us further to guilt, shame, and regret, but to draw us to repentance so we could be restored and redeemed. In many ways, we are prodigal children living independent from God, but all we prove when we think we know better is how much we need the Lord's grace, mercy, and forgiveness to survive.

Quality time with the Lord is all about deepening our personal relationship with Him and dying to ourselves. Whether we care to admit it, God does not need us. We need Him—all day, every day! Only a fool would proclaim himself a follower of Jesus Christ yet find no value in prayer. Thus, we are wise to sift truth from God's Word to counter the lies we have chosen to believe about prayer. The Father's arms are open wide to welcome us home, but we must come to our senses, repent of our sins, and reconcile our hearts to Him like prodigal children (Luke 15:11-32).

That does not mean becoming proficient in prayer will be easy. Learning spiritual disciplines is difficult at first, but the blessings which await those who remedy their excuses with the truth of Scripture are infinite. I have never felt closer to the Lord than during this season of self-examination and conviction regarding my lack of faith in the power of prayer. Nevertheless, the real work now begins, and I pray we overcome our prayer struggles and allow the Spirit to ignite revival in our hearts so we no longer feel distant from the Lord but forever close to His heart.

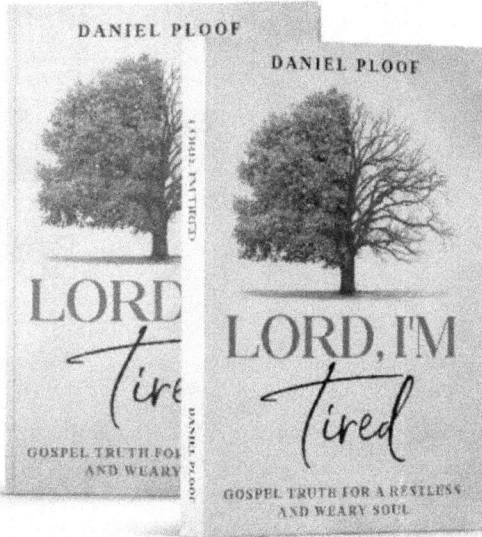

LORD, I'M TIRED
Gospel Truth for a Restless and Weary Soul

Why am I so overwhelmed by fear, doubt, and worry? How can I resist giving up when the storms of life tempt me to lose faith? What is God's plan and purpose for my life when it feels like the walls are closing in around me? Why do I feel so tired and helpless, crushed by the weight of pain and confusion?

"Lord, I'm Tired," unpacks twenty issues which consume our minds, directing our attention toward God's Word for answers to life's trials. Whether enslaved to sin or struggling to resist temptation, we can discover hope and healing in the absolute truth of holy Scripture which casts light into the darkness of our hearts. All we need is to focus our attention on Jesus Christ to find rest for our weary souls and discover the peace of God which surpasses all understanding (Phil. 4:7).

Target Audience: Men, Women, and Teens.

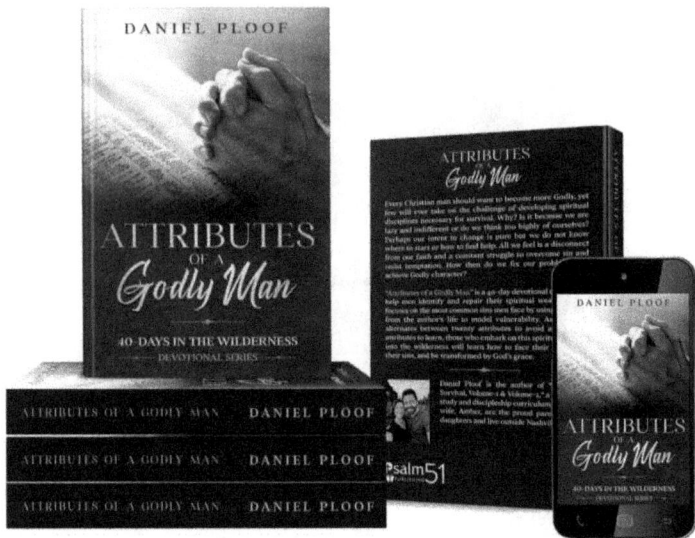

ATTRIBUTES OF A GODLY MAN

Every Christian man should want to become more Godly, yet few will ever take on the challenge of developing spiritual disciplines necessary for survival. Why? Is it because we are lazy and indifferent, or do we think too highly of ourselves? Perhaps our intent to change is pure but we do not know where to start or how to find help. All we feel is a disconnect from our faith and a constant struggle to overcome sin and resist temptation. How then do we fix our problems and achieve Godly character?

"Attributes of a Godly Man" is a 40-day devotional designed to help men identify and repair their spiritual weaknesses. It focuses on the most common sins men face daily by using examples from the author's life to model vulnerability. As each day alternates between twenty attributes to avoid and twenty attributes to learn, those who embark on this spiritual journey into the wilderness will learn how to face their fears, own their sins, and be transformed by God's grace.

Target Audience: Men, Women, and Teens.

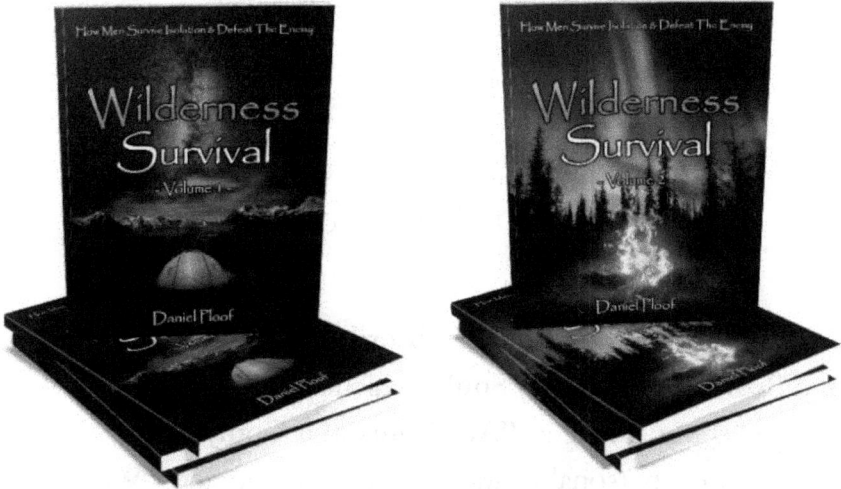

WILDERNESS SURVIVAL
Volume-1 & Volume-2

Men's Bible Study / Discipleship Curriculum

Embark on a journey of survival training deep in the spiritual wilderness of isolation where few men dare to venture. Explore forty personal issues every man deals with in his life and marriage. Embrace the ultimate accountability challenge to become the man, husband, and father God calls you to be by transforming your life and changing your behavior.

"Wilderness Survival" is all about building Godly spiritual disciplines and surrendering to God's authority by examining your heart and filtering it through the absolute truth of His Word. The more you learn to guard your mind, the greater chance you will have of surviving the wilderness seasons of life and marriage, restoring the joy of your salvation, and defeating the enemy once and for all.

Target Audience: Men in relationships; preparatory for singles.

About The Author

Daniel Ploof is the author of **"Lord, I'm Tired: Gospel Truth for a Restless and Weary Soul,"** which helps Christians overcome trials and spiritual fatigue; **"Attributes of a Godly Man,"** a 40-day devotional on personal character development; and **"Wilderness Survival, Vol-1 & Vol-2,"** a 40-week Bible study and discipleship curriculum designed to help men overcome isolation and become more godly husbands and fathers.

He is also the founder of **"Wilderness Survival Training,"** a resource platform designed to help Christian men and women find wisdom and discernment in God's Word. For more information and access to reflections, devotionals, and discipleship resources, please visit: **https://www.journeyintothewilderness.com**.

Daniel has been married to the love of his life and best friend, Amber, for over twenty-three years. They live outside Nashville, TN, and are the proud parents of four amazing daughters who are their greatest treasures this side of heaven.

www.ingramcontent.com/pod-product-compliance
Lightning Source LLC
Chambersburg PA
CBHW060320050426
42449CB00011B/2569